TABLE OF CONTENTS

Feature Poet:

Larry D. Thomas

Poetry:

Art:

There were the distances that enfolded every feature of the landscape and there was the force of geologic time, out there somewhere, the string grids of excavators searching for weathered bone.

— Don DeLillo, *Point Omega*

San Pedro River Review
Vol. 8 No. 1   Spring 2016

San Pedro River Review (SPRR) Vol. 8 No. 1, Spring 2016
Blue Horse Press, Redondo Beach, California, United States.

COVER ART: "Terlingua, Toward the Chisos Range" courtesy
of Blue Horse Press Archives (2012). Larry D. Thomas author
photo by Carol Rowe DeBender, Houston, Texas.

EDITORS & PUBLISHERS: Jeffrey and Tobi Alfier

SPRR (ISSN 1944-5954) is a semiannual publication of poetry
and art, published by Blue Horse Press. It is named for the
ancient river that flows north from the mountains of Sonora,
Mexico, into Arizona. The website associated with SPRR is
www.bluehorsepress.com.

Community of Literary Magazines & Presses

San Pedro River Review

Vol. 8 No. 1   Spring 2016

Texas Canyon

(Arizona)

Larry D. Thomas

By the thousands
and for miles,
like pebbles

worn smooth
by centuries
of swift rivers,

huge boulders
dozens of feet
in diameter

pepper the hillsides
and arroyos,
as if young gods

just dumped
their bags of marbles,
sure they'll still be there

when they return
from their afternoon,
million-year naps,

wiping sleep
from their eyes
and yawning.

Great Horned Owl

Larry D. Thomas

On the slope of an arroyo,
on the gnarled branches
of a centenarian mesquite,

it roosts. The rocky
ground beneath the tree
is strewn with the bone-

pellets of scores
of black-tailed jackrabbits.
It's blessed with at best

two hard decades
of existence absent
even a millisecond

of sentiment.
Deep into the boundless,
desert darkness,

but to claim its morsel
of bleakness,
it pours its song.

Winter Solstice

(Kokernot 06 Ranch, Brewster County, Texas)

Larry D. Thomas

A late December blast
of Canadian air
has left the pasture
a naked corpse
laid out and tagged
on the stainless steel
gurney of a morgue.

What birds remain
rend the cobalt sky
like shards of dark sleet.
The lowing cattle,
still as scarecrows on sticks
stuck deep in the ground,
loom on the horizon

as if suspended
in the red-orange
Popsicle of the sunset.
It's as if they know,
by whatever wisdom
the god of beasts
has accorded them,

that the night will fall
and they can't stop it;
that all they can do
is watch as its pearl-
moon of icy fire
rises in the lacquered
pupils of their stares.

Permian Basin

Larry D. Thomas

Dust is the common denominator
of the fractions of their lives.
In spring, when the sandstorms come,
the townsfolk, just to breathe,
filter their mouths, nostrils with kerchiefs.

Even as they live, it fills
every orifice of their eked out souls,
reducing interment to redundancy.
Down the curbs of dead downtowns,
it rages in red rivers.

Films of it blanket the cribs of infants,
toughening their gums on grit.
For recreation, the townsfolk pilgrim
to Monahans Sandhills State Park,
to tan sand towering seventy feet

in dunes which run for miles,
where children bury children for fun.
It's no wonder the growling
belly of survival here's
girded with the belt of the Bible.

Balmorhea Lake

(far West Texas)

Larry D. Thomas

In his dream,
even the night wind
is deferent, reverent
with perfect stillness.

The night is moonless.
The surface of the lake,
smooth as a film of silver,
mirrors the cloudless

desert sky. It's as if
the heavens entire
reside there,
filling the lake

with blinding brightness.
He sees fishermen
casting their nets
and dragging them ashore,

nets sagging and fraying
with thousands of stars
still raging, though billions
of years dead.

Bells
(Alpine, Texas)
Larry D. Thomas

On the flanks
of "A" Mountain
on the south side of town,

towers a three-level belfry
fashioned of native stone.
It's the eastern of two towers

abutting the sanctuary
of Our Lady of Peace
Catholic Church.

On Sunday mornings,
the sound of the bells
drifts down to the town

like sonorous dust,
swirling about the houses,
seeping through open windows,

gracing everything it touches
with a sheen-like film
of sacred hymns.

Terlingua Ghost Town

Larry D. Thomas

Today, I rode with a friend
down to Terlingua, one of the few
places left in the country
where one may live anonymously,
secludedly off-the-grid. Ever
unincorporated, it has haunted me

since I first visited it as a child.
The mouths of the old mine shafts
are black, spewing bats at dusk,
wooing men like the jasmine-
scented chanting of Sirens.
The locals speak of the foolhardy

who, succumbing to the urge
to descend, lose their footing,
tumble down the rough,
cold walls of cinnabar,
and crumple like puppets
beneath slackened strings.

From their benches on "The Porch"
of the Terlingua Trading Company,
the locals whisper, facing east,
growing silent as the darkness
nibbling the Chisos, rubbling
the crayons of sundown to dust.

The Visitation
(All Souls' Day, *Los Días de Los Muertos*)
Larry D. Thomas

The chilled cemetery air
is redolent with *mole negro*,
tamales, *pan de los muertos*,

and burning incense. Darkness
is falling on paths aglow
with marigolds and candles

to light the way for the dead.
It is 6 p.m., and the bells
begin to ring to summon

the sacred spirits. A bonfire
lifts burning cinders to the sky.
At Clemente's grave, the cross

and kneeling countenances
of Irene and Helga cast
long shadows. In due time,

Clemente's spirit will arrive,
so palpable it could easily
be mistaken for the wind.

Pecos, Texas

(for Walt McDonald)

Larry D. Thomas

Even the distant, blue Davis Mountains
one must squint in the sun to see
are dry as bleached skulls. Though home
of the world's first rodeo,

it's now known for its vineyards
and its world renown cantaloupes
which top the gourmet offerings
of candlelit smorgasbords

with sweet wedges of West Texas sunsets.
A few months ago, ten miles to the north,
while stretching my legs and wandering
near a fence of barbed wire, a two-inch thorn

on a branch of mesquite several years dead
yet perfectly preserved, pierced
not only my New Balance sole
but also the calloused flesh of my heel,

the land's way of reminding me why
cattle here far outnumber people
and judges, mumbling their gutless sentences,
pale against the justice of the wind.

"Cornfield, Indian Farm Near Tuba City, Arizona, in Rain, 1941"
(photograph by Ansel Adams)
Larry D. Thomas

He saw
with the eyes of hawks
covered with black cloth.
Of darkness

in brush and mesa,
he fashioned
broad horizontals
to frame

his dark verticals
of rows of dead cornstalks.
He etched each corn leaf
in stark relief,

a dark divining rod
arched in its rendezvous
with flooded earth
shiny as hammered silver.

The Day We Split in Two – Entering the USA

You'll learn English and the proper way to say, "Yes, Sir!"

Lisha Adela García

At midnight, fleeing my father
in the back seat of a Rambler
station wagon, life escapes
into my mother's bruises
as a sullen driver speeds us north.

A palm of trumpet
notes blooms from the radio,
lodges into her clavicle,
breath upon breath.

At high speed, around
mountain curves
and miles of gravel
we hope to cross
the Sierra Madre before dawn.

Rancor for dreams left in the rains of Mexico City settle into her eyes.
How will I survive this lower altitude
split in two,
our spirits vaporizing
into the rocks of the cordillera?

The cigarette smoke paths
she still craves in sleep
bind her fear – tattoo her face.

From this day forward,
her words,
full of hidden ordnance.

Petrichor

Jim Natal

Yes, there is a word for it,
that first fragrance of rain rising up from the pavement.

With eyes closed, you can smell
sidewalks recently sprinkled; toes of shoes go dark with damp.

There's no term for the scent of kindling dry—
fields, forest floors, chaparral arroyos that are imminent tinder;

brush crackles at each step,
straw in a broom wanting to sweep clean, begging for lightning.

Year upon year of no precipitation,
no snow pack, aquifers drawn down, the ground like sunken
cheeks.

It's come to this, the Anasazi choice:
crops to eat or water to drink, crops to eat or water to drink,

the drought chant before leaving.

Tour Guide Tells How He Grew Up With This Dam on the Colorado River

Carol Hamilton

Three months on this retirement job
and I can walk backwards fast
and talk without stumbling.
I can tell all about the turbines,
the low waters now,
and this maybe leading
to another exit one day
like in the time of the Anazasi.
I tell how many floors
the elevators go to
and about the real green grass
down there that just looks like
green paint from up here,
and how the boys keep it mowed
and trimmed like it's
the lawn at the White House.
I get to going on how we kids
used to hang out here,
in and out, in the old days,
about our mischief and how Bill
jumped off the dam on a dare
and just got locked up
for one night with a scolding
and a talk to his folks.
Probably be in for life today!

Well, times change,
and I'm still talking
when they thank me and head off
on to more of their hectic travel.
But I got to tell them,
those were really the days!
And if anyone in these parts
had more fun as a kid
or has a better gig
for his retirement days,
well, you can just show him
to me. If you can, I'll maybe
be taking a plunge into
these sitting-still waters myself!

Tyuonyi Pueblo

Bandelier National Monument, New Mexico
Steve Dieffenbacher

From above, it is a fallen isolation of stones,

concentric circles near cottonwoods hiding the creek.

Inside the fallen walls, grasses bend to the times.

Rim-top trees and cones define earth with shadows;

wind cracks like glass, an old argument.

Among the rocks, voices recall former duties,

every child reborn in a sadness of dust.

Through weed-grown kivas, rotting ladders gape,

the cave to the underworld turning brittle-gray

with unrequited leavings.

Rohan Garg, **Ladder**

Listen,

S.J. Dunning

My first word wasn't a bang.
No man's rib was taken for the sake of it—

      and I'm not just saying that
      to establish agency.

I never crossed the Bering Land Bridge
to arrive in Clovis, New Mexico like a fluted-point projectile—
there's no salmon bones and awls
and beads in me.

I can't claim any of those abstract lines
buried by the ash of Mt. Mazama: paintings
from before Christ was born.

I wasn't, in other words, the first artist
to occupy this land, or an innovator full of hunter's rage.
I didn't say *micro-blades for butchery* before each had a name.

Sinkers, gorges, hooks, spears for fishing, and even more salmon
never drifted through my origin.

Pithouses don't village my Cold Springs
sites—there are no such sites
of which I can speak.

Drawings of men and dogs
chasing mountain-sheep are not prolific
on the rocks of my nation.

I don't have a South Dakota story either,
or early armor, or a maul
for shaping wood.

I'm not accessorized like an Early Riverine
Barbie: hairpins, pendants, dice.

My loved ones won't bury me
with everything I cherish.

        That was a long time ago.

You can find me after 1700—well after wild horses
thundered their way across this
vast plateau,

after their war-painted bodies turned to steel
on the hill that makes me shift
into low gear.

The one on the other side
of the wide river.

I'm angry about muses—pompous little playwrights,
refusing to translate what they whisper late at night
when I smoke or soak in a tub.

Look at this photograph I've been studying for decades:
a father's boots, a mother's shadow
next to mine.

Look under the rattlesnake rocks of my alphabet, far into the brush
of my pet doe's disappearance, in the cracks
in pebbles eyes become

after too many cardboard years.

That's not to say I'm mute in the slice of petrified Elm
that looks like me, in profile, when I wear my hair up.
Or that I can't hear the sound of an ancient dam
of ice cracking.

Sometimes, I even want to get into my black car
and drive through the desert—back to before
lava licked this valley, back to before ribs,
back to the source of the static
on my stereo.

It's like I've been there before
and miss it.

It's like what if all the whispering I hear
is from a theater for ghosts,
and I'm waiting in line?

> *Can you hear me?*
> *Can you hear me now?*

> I've been wondering
> for a while.

Rural Utah: I

Lisa Fay Coutley

Finding a bed—a place
prey stops its shot body
to treat a wound, halting
the trail of blood—is bad
news for any tracker. Chalk
hearts drawn along the curb
I balance beam each morning
while puppy pines for the end
of his leash have outlasted all
of my feelings this winter.
Another year without sex
that lasts longer than the time
it takes to erase your name
with rain. Sidewalk slabs poured
where once there were needles
for the kill to bed down, leaves
for blood to lead the way. Love
in any language not our own
means more. You were dear to me
as sleep or fire. Homing bones.
Injured meat. Wound to end hunger.

Bosque

Jan Selving

Among the trees of heaven, coyote
willow, saltgrass, tamarisk, sedge
and cattail, false indigo, wolf berry,
fleabane, yerba mansa, spike rush,
and thorny Russian Olive a call frays
across the river. Seconds later
the answer's long, arcing wail floats
across the cul-de-sacs and stucco
mazes lining the bluff behind me.

      On this narrow path,
my dog pulls at her leash. She wants
to run, catch the crows who launch
seconds before she can get up to speed.
There are holes in the forest since the fire,
arson or maybe just some kids playing
with matches. Underbrush so dry
it didn't take long to catch, the wind
to whip it into an orange blaze
that shook down the cottonwoods.
200 acres in Albuquerque, 1000
farther up the Rio Grande. It followed
the oxbow then moved south
toward Las Lunas. Embers paved
the droughted bluffs. It was,

as Lorca said, *the time of parched
things* when panic filled a bucket
a garden hose, meager jets soaking
walls and shingles. A store owner
hauled his inventory to a parking lot.
In a grainy news photo, he's standing
among stacked cages of dogs, cats,
gerbils and rabbits, all blurred forms
inside those cages. Smoldering
nests and burrows displaced muskrat
jumping mouse, gopher and cottontail.
Chorus frogs, whiptails, blunt-nosed
bull snake abandoned the riverbank.

My dog finds a mound, matted
and dusted with pollen. I envy her
ecstatic frenzy as she dives through
black fugues, pushes her nose deeper
into the stink of coyote ambush.
They would've surrounded, charmed it,
invited it to play, their muzzles pressed
to the ground, faking submission. I clear
flies from a milky iris. It catches light
now and then like labradorite, a faint
contraction beneath the lens. The city left
a few dead trees for hawks and bald eagles.
They'll sit there all afternoon, sometimes
well into the evening.

Witchery Wish

Natalie Young

In the book and on the coast, she conjures
thunder, lightning jetting the line
where ocean meets air. Not just drops—slices of rain
sloop the sudden dark sky.
How unfair,
the ability to command storms,
when she practically lives on water.

First one tooth falls on the counter
with a click. Two and a half more
jiggle out with little effort, a few minor
crunchy shards. It's an unconscious sign:
life feels like poultry without heads. The gaps bloody,
but painless. This time there's no argument
with dream's interpretation.

A hidden someone in these dusty mountains
should mix a potion, gather clouds
into shark-grey cotton candy, force
the sky to spew the tears of a mammal,
salty elements worthy of scandal.

A dog sidles up to me, holds one long black hair
on its tongue. The hair is not her own.
It should be confiscated, saved
for later ritual,
cleansing or vengeance. For now, it prances
over linoleum, droops off
either side of the jowls.

The math of pumps and makeup tips
pile on the side of the bed. Shiny
ads with fuchsia lips, neglected swatches
of fragrance and trial moisture. This week
I don't want to know how to be
radiant. This week I don't believe in anything
I can't taste.

Labor Day

Shaun Asbury

Too close to Tucson
to shut it down, we teeter
on the long weekend, the shortened
week fully dressed as we wouldn't
for this terrain, as they have,
moving farther inland to sack some
puppy out of the puppy. At this height,
the party's over, though
tell it to the bottles with butts
at their bottoms clinking
like toasts. I want something profound
& ordinary as hope on a holiday,
habits that can't be broken or else.
But I can't wake them up, even
in the sugar of the rising sun,
that cooled drinkable liquid
of light glistening off Lake Powell
like wind chimes, they labor,
preferring my silence on such matters
as the shore shaking off
its slumber beneath the beached
houseboat a-strummin' to the early bird
slaloming over fast glass, soothing
as waterfalls & whale calls. The stars

are dead at any height, though
an hour ago a stelliferous sky, the water
a body at a wake. For three days,
sudden sleep, & simple. Monday morning,
I am coming down as they come back
scattered dark bits of a dawning, legs
like dust storms side-steppin' thorny
pink bushes, glowing buffalo grass.
We'll start up twin motors. To push off,
& back.

Marilyn Stablein, **Garage**

Two Men

Paul Christensen

Someone enters the store at closing time
and waits for service.
The twilight falls across the floor
like lava pouring from the sun.
His shoes are globes of light,
his trousers singed with embers
of the afternoon. His hands
keep altering the shadows
behind him. He has become a flame
as he stands patiently, fingers
tapping on the counter, listening
intently for the sound of footsteps.

But the only other living soul
is in the basement standing in the dark,
talking softly to himself.
He can't seem to sort his thoughts
and stock the heaps of unsold goods
he is responsible for. He feels
stuck in the dark, lost in it,
like a swimmer who keeps clawing
at the sea that swallows him.
He hears the man above
and cries out, but can't be heard.

My Pride of Barbados

Marian Haddad

bushes popping buds, especially the full-grown
shrub the lawman's assistant once mowed down

—not a very good year, or the following seasons,
but now it is full-bodied, bodacious, demanding

attention—*fire on the river* (no river here) but the grass
is wet—and lush in its post-rain verdancy, popping

-orange petals against a nearly-blood-rust
on the inside of a bud. Proud

color graces the yard, the taller bush's stalks reach
toward slate-blue sky; the shorter, stouter bush,

newly alive, fat with foliage,
proud in its best garb

***

—The window, if you look out,
brings all this color in—and then

the vine that grows along the back
wooden fence—fat, as well, this year, heavy

—and orange trumpets color the grass
—fall, like day and the heavy

heavy hanging
orange-trumpets-on-a-sleepy-vine

—there, cover the edge   of grass.

The Pepper Tree

Gina Valdés

Survivor of gusts
of wind, fire, smoke,
lightning, hailstorms,
drought.

Deep-rooted, thick-skinned,
bushy-haired Brazilian pepper—
my aging family's shield
from East San Diego sun's
daily arrows—

convalesces in patio,
cracked and bare, limbs torn
and flung to the ground by wrath
of an all-night Santa Ana.

Victor the gardener who says
he's from Oaxacalifornia,
prunes pepper, smiles
at moist bark, predicts
shade by summer.

On waking, I look out
at a new vista: stark
tree with exposed gold bark,

newly visible hills
of neighing, bronco-riding,
gas-guzzling, flag-waving,
KSON country town

with habit of glowering
flame red, cycling
grief black, born-again green.

January: hot
windstorms, cold squalls.
The Pacific pounding our houses.

Years-long drought followed by
month-long deluge,
slick mud.

My family with roots
in this and other soils
begins to dislodge,
our tendrils loosening
their grip.

With budding green tongues
the pepper announces spring

while I soak in my living room
flooded with gold light.

Tumbleweed Picking

Chera Hammons

The yard is lousy
with dark stars of them,
trails of them left where their predecessors traveled
the year before on their inexorable journeys
to ditches and barbed wire fences.
Most of those that came before are flattened and burned by now,
but with the rain those tough shoots began
to push up the cracked ground,
lifting flat chunks of tan dirt in their miniature branches
while their red and white legs shook below.
They ruin the neighborhood for every other plant.
My salvia, strawberries, thyme have young tumbleweeds
nestling right in the centers of them.
They spread like oil stains over the land, in dark patches.
I pluck out whole forests of them—
the earlier the better, before they thicken and prick
the picker. Their young bodies, I leave
drying and blackening to show where I've been.
I have become obsessed with them,
see them on my eyelids like the ghosts of fireworks,
small sparkles and bursts, wide at the bottoms.

I often go to bed with hands red
and swollen with brutality,
but no matter how many I rip
from the sand, more appear.
Strange to think that something that grows
with such tenacity
exists for the purpose of detaching,
rolling to the wind's whim.
When it rains, I watch the tiny plants I have pulled
washing down the rivulets,
each reaching with arms dried
and spiderlike, and one dried white taproot
trailing like regret.

Fire May Flow Like Flood

James Toupin

Buds on the tendrils
of the climbing vine
that winds the way
up the sun-scoured slope,
the houses claim
the view the ground once owned.

Now that living
need not crowd the oasis,
the city reaches
out, borne on the death
of dragons, to
entangle the high desert.

The human once
struggled through this country
where people now
root down the foundations
for sprouting walls
and roofs, raising shadows.

Vistas lure their
gaze away from the peaks.
Yet from mountains,
the long-forgotten said,
the bird will come,
servant of the on high.

Eyes on it all,
the bird will ride air's surge
to where a catch
in the rise sets its wings
beating the heat-
charged heaven to thunder.

More Romantic in Past Tense

Kaitlin LaMoine Martin

Edinburg is best viewed through the rearview mirror,
my friend's husband tells me. But the pelicans returning

each autumn are lovely, and my mother keeps writing
about the anhinga she saw here last November.

If Edinburg had a mascot it'd be a birder, styled
in safari gear, 800mm lens and tripod slung over

his shoulder, binoculars bouncing as he walks
the wetlands. With careful positioning, he avoids

runoff to the west, stadium lights to the east. Angled just
right, he fancies himself somewhere beautiful.

Large as it is, you can't claim anything in Texas,
let alone the Valley. There are 75 state birds. And stray

dogs are the new squirrel. It's kind of a bad poem.
The one you revise over and over, putting in party store

after raspa stand after taquería after carwash, finally
combining all four signs into one, written in both Spanish

and English. You can still see that first draft under layered
architecture, the way raspa syrup inevitably bleeds through

the paper cone. But it's got heart, a slow beat, looping
around Freddy Gonzales park each night, browsing the aisles

of the last Blockbuster store in the nation, folding laundry, Sunday
mornings, at the Spin Center, while everyone else is in church.

Please do not let me forget

Megan Merchant

the first time I looped the bird feeder over the branch
and had to chose which category of seeds
to add in its beaker-thin tube—

Santa Ana, stratus, estuary—
hummingbird, robin, blue jay.

Not hawk. Not raven.

Please do not let me forget the barred wing-feather
that ambled down the drive
before the husk of storm,

a child's hands unable to collapse
around such quick-lightness.

The type of feather that could make a quill, an arrow,
replace the worry-stone that heavies hands,
climbs the latticework of a gale.

A feather that falls from a lack of water
and sways into a pond
is a song.

Can be dried and bunched
for sweeping.

Please do not let the quiet, dust-handprint
smudge from the surface of wood—
its tiny net, its ghost breath,

knowing too well—brevity,
trying preserve and hold it
all the same.

Reformation

Taylor Leigh D'Amico

Among rotting leaves, hidden
in brush, the bird's broken belly
opens to gray sky. Fragile, rapt.

Barely bigger than an egg, its head
lies tilted back, bearing
only the lower beak, trapped
in final song.

Through outstretched neck and open throat,
a purple channel— like a worm
dried by light—beached
at the surface, detached
from blood, warmth.

From throat-shaft, the body rests —
wings spread as fletchings at an arrow's end
now fallen from the last grand arc.

Gently, I sweep him into a pot — all feathers
in terracotta — then pour and pack in fresh earth.
I take on the finch's song,

and still my hand on the loam,
feel for a pulse. Then with soiled palms
dig deep for seeds, meet
with heat of tempered shell.

Where Desert Meets Ocean

John Grey

I hike up to the cliff edge,
follow the myth
of two lovers turned into azaleas by a witch
except there are none of
the blood-red bushes growing here.
The soil is too pallid.
A few palm warblers decorate the low scrub.

Down below, a strip of sand
fills with terns,
a brief diversion from a sea
that has never seemed more inaccessible
as it dips its toes in sand
a hundred feet below,
then retreats through gaps in rocks
all the way to the horizon.

Sure, the view from here is far
but it's also slow-witted,
a briny flat-top rippled by wind-currents,
a yellow sheen, empty sky.

I don't think the fabled pair
were in love at all really.
Probably just another mismatched couple,
desert and salt water,
uncomfortable with each other,
joined at the shoreline hip
but forever keeping their distance.

The cypresses are dying.
The waves slag off some kelp.
That sun's as hot as
any sphere of burning plasma
has a right to be.
One good leap from cooling liquid,
I feel myself burning.
That's not a caution,
just a fact.

One-track Mind Conflicted

Tim Staley

Josh and I hiked yesterday
to where the Rio Grande swallows the Red,
600 cubic feet of fast water
hardly coerced by 30 more.

Two kayakers pull out a half klik
upriver from our camp and fling
their boats on their backs and zip
the mile straight up to the rim of the canyon.
There's a cooler of cold beer in their car
and they're not going home, they're going to the Chama,
the Yampa, the Colorado, the Buffalo,
the Chattooga, the Coosa, the Tallapoosa...

Josh and I are quiet for days
like the black basalt boulders
that slowly sink in the Rio's banks
like dying worms with one-track minds
that know they should disintegrate
but keep on digging anyway.

I know I should return to where I started
but need to keep feeling this brush
of pine needles against my cheek, this wisp
of lightning, these battered clouds
facing off the New Mexico sun.

A Walk in the Foothills After Ten Years of Drought

Kyce Bello

From here it is as if nothing
has changed.
                Beneath
the piñons there are tufts

of moss the size
of a half dollar resting

amidst the scattering

of pine cones that didn't bear
nut-meat last year

and haven't for some time.

Perhaps you've heard
that quote from Whitman

about how all one needs

is the green world

            growing alongside you.
But what of the world falling
before us?

I could sit all day in this circle
of desert moss, brown

and green-brown clusters

perched atop what we call soil,
greening when the green time comes,

       retreating
when it is past.

Circuits

Rillito Wash, Tucson
William Cordeiro

I.

Blue glare of noon has swallowed each faint star.
Dew shrivels on a thorn. A shrill wren cries.
Sun loots the darkened mountains down ravines
through jagged folds. As shadows disagree
along the rocks, each prickly-pear swells pink;
all distance melts in light. Each lax grain holds
before it's chafed beyond the boulders' reach.
The red sand burns. Dust torques the river's tracks,
and faint—above such sharp, denuded forms—
one hawk lists over and the whole day turns.

II.

I run the rim dug in where water's rushed,
a scab-bright dusk above exposed dry bed.
Beside mesquite the tailwinds rend, I face
sun-racing clouds which build a bruising head
in pace with my own steps, then leap like thoughts
along a lightning's crack—
                                                    I hear no sound
when looking down the path until I crash
into the whiplash of a lizard's tail
that twitches, flailing, bloody in the flash
as floods rip waste across the twisting wash.

Quick night encroaches, and the slow light fails.

The Crack

Jack Granath

A raven on a tangled branch
Somewhere not too far from Ghost Ranch
Leans into the failing light,
Starts stiffly up, and falls to flight,
Becomes less live, less really there,
A simple print against the air;
It goes from fleshing out a tree
Into a new nonentity,
From body to its deficit,
The torn-off silhouette of it,
And with one blast of its black tongue
Drags watcher and the watched along.

Six Storms

Steve Wilson

Storms flower, the skies
blackening to slate. Nightjars
dive into an echo.

***

Rain thunders in, all teeth and bone.

***

Autumn storms conjure
a second spring –
fall greens, blooms,
in spite of itself.

***

Under lowering skies, summer
growls and glowers, then goes.

***

– the eloquence of mist at storm's edge –

***

storms
descended – evening
all day.

Monday After a Stormy Sunday

David Thomas

A day washed clear
        by yesterday's rain
leaves hang weary
        but still green
after a long hot summer
        clouds
        bearing
        the colors
of storm
build in the southwest
        the river
        sparkles
with afternoon
        sun
and all that's really
        needed
can be found
        in the quiet
        nexus
of sunlight
and leaf shadow.

Highway 85

David Chorlton

A desert prison lies at rest
beneath sweeps of light
that break through changing clouds
on the day after rain
                and wet
shadows cling to the rock
formations on the bright side
of the highway
            as sun picks out
remaining pools and vegetation
stripped to its winter core
                  on land
pulling free from a harrier's grip.

End of the Season at the Helibase

Jerry D. Mathes II

Late afternoon
and the wind
comes up—
the still rotors flex and hum.

Two flight suits hang
from the bulkhead,
swish and kick, empty,
on the erratic wind.

Summer days fold
on themselves—one
shrinking more than the last,
stretching out the fall
nights without fire.

Seven of us sit
in a circle
talking about everything
except home.

From the base
I can see the smoke column
as it fades like gun blued
winter mist over the far buttes.

I pick my teeth
with a mesquite thorn.
Juniper berries fall—
too dry to ferment.

I cough up red dirt
from rotor wash.
It fills my nose, my ears.
Through the summer, I hear
your voice in the fire,
in the rattling brush.

Some nights, lying in my sleeping bag,
the air carries the taste of you,
not dry, but like the first fall rain
that hardly settles the powdery dust.

To a Blackhawk

Reuven Goldfarb

who settled on the crown of the highest tree,
with a great flutter of wings

Do not suppose, because I am supine,
that I am helpless, or imagine that some prey,
till now unknown, has drifted downstream
to your hunting ground. I am a predator
as well as you, as able to defend
myself at need, as willing to reach out
and to consume what I require to live.
Yet now I am contemplative, content
to watch the shining moon and glowing planet
farther still; attend to crickets' cry,
the croak of birds, and flowing waters rippling
past my resting feet, below this rocky hill.

Quail Hunt, Lincoln Co., OK, 1982

Benjamin Myers

The Johnson grass is like a yellow flame
beneath a thin glass dome. My grandfather
this morning wades into that fire,
his 20 gauge draped open in the crook
of his elbow, like a bird he's already shot.
I follow his orange plaid hunting jacket
through waist-high blades of scouring, blonded grass
to pet the dog he's brought for nosing up
the birds from bare and brushy upwards rush
of scrub. I know by the time we cross
this frozen creek again the shells he's spent
will bulge my pocket like a bullfrog's throat.
This man was born before this land was a state
and now begins to knee his way into
the high grass of his last ten years, not yet
frail, not yet waning down to elbow
and kneecap on a hospice bed, still strong
as cedar root in hard red earth. The dog
noses a sudden flash of bobwhites up,
like a handful of dirt clods flung
against the cold clear dome of pre-snow sky.
And some may say to shoot them down is brutal,
but I already know that, in a place
that's mostly sky, to shoot a bird back down
to earth is just a way to keep the rest
of all we've got from rising to follow
and falling up toward that dead-cold,
forever distant, cracked and bluish dome.

Upon Leaving *The House of Dreams*
Casa de Suenos

Marian Haddad

The wild sadness
in leaving this sky—
the sun   the stars

set against
pitch black—
the desert night
—dust kicking up
as I drive

—dust, air, sky, night
stars that shimmer
in phosphorescent light—

windows open—
I ride, looking out
and up
        at this
        great sky—

        and the stars

        they seem closer
        tonight
        than far

and the breeze
blowing through

this corridor—

ocotillo, purple sage,
oleander, pink
and white

these yellow buds
of the desert
birds of paradise

the yucca plants' stalks
raised up in the light.

First published in *Wildflower. Stone.* (Pecan Grove Press, 2011)

My Mother's Eyes

Loretta Diane Walker

I fuss with supper
stuffed in white Styrofoam.
Mama parks her wheelchair
at the oak table.
Diabetes made her legs ghosts.
Both amputated below the knee.

She stares beyond the backyard,
cuddles inside her sweater,
hugs heat and layers of years
against the cliff of her breasts.
The distant gaze in her glaucoma eyes is her Oz.
This kitchen, my Kansas.

I feel myself whirling in a wind of desire.
I want to crawl inside her mind,
view her unwrinkled memories, see what reels
are spinning in the theatre of her thoughts.

Perhaps she is a child running in a long field of wildflowers?
Bony body draped in a humble dress.
Hair styled in cornrows.
Face bumping against the sun's chest of heat.

Perhaps she returned to the powdery-colored cotton
fields of east Texas where she moves
with a sack strapped around her shoulder?
Walking, bent, picking from open bolls,
singing in her soft soprano voice?
Singing until a crew of stars tunnels
through debris of darkness,
ignites small torches of light in a summer sky.

I feel her spirits sprinting, *Going Up Yonder*
with gates constructed of pearls,
walls crafted with jasper, sapphire,
streets paved with gold.

I want to write on the wide window,
Here is your Emerald City.
Come back. Sit with me in this moment.

I bump her chair with my knee.
Do you want all shrimp?

Mohave

Doug Anderson

Stars come one by one
like turtle hatchlings
and thicken in a black sky
until you can almost see by them.
This is what I want to give you.
Rain sweetened mesquite
and in the morning, lizards
razoring sun-bleached stucco
into black line drawings.
Mourning doves. Wildflowers
in the foothills. Jesus was not only
tempted in the desolation
but restored. A demon
stripper, a devil with a money clip,
nothing compared to the way
the flash flood comes suddenly,
new sculpts the arroyo and subsides.
In the silence after coyotes
come in the dark to drink.
This is what I want to give you.

Yuma Sunrise

Chila Woychik

When the night heavies down, and memories
shadow dance against a window etched
with moonlight, a desert stiff with thorns—
I ask the deathly swelter,
can I write your sand?

When a bat weaves across the birthing
daybreak, pre-dawn blue, pink-streaked clouds
and scrubby brush surrounds it all—
I tell the silent tan and brown,
you should not keep quiet at a bird's fall.

And when white has crested, eye of sun
between the pass (it surges quickly),
shadows trail behind me, this great power—
I bow before it and
a seagull cries.

Lost in the Sonora, Sunset of the Fourth Day

golden shovel on a haiku by Ann Howells

David Meischen

Along the moonlit arroyo, cactus
spines, the bristle of edges, a screech-owl
calling from juniper shadow. Day retreats,
sky a bruise deep
and darkening into
cold, into dream, the sleep of saguaro
prickling at wakefulness. A nest
of lizard eggshells, a lacing of snow.
The escarpment shivers, dusts
the wind with grit, the
fissure scar long healed beneath the glowing yuccas.

The Way to Sanco

Susan Rooke

The ruined road is luminous as vellum
beneath a vault of stars. It wanders
through draws, across the spines of steep hills,
and to walk it, stumbling in darkness over ruts
and badger dens, is to know this land by feel
alone, by the creases folded into stern earth.
Here are volcanoes extinct for perhaps
40 million years, and standing on their rough iron
shoulders you can gaze unobstructed
at the night sky. You will see the cold burn
of the spangled universe gazing back at you,
all those reflective, shining eyes on a far shore.
So much black water in between to row
ourselves across, as if the prehistoric ocean
that once drowned these rocky plains and knobs
was drawn up by a younger, willful moon,
tides forced to ebb ever higher.
Not knowing where, or how, to stop.

Shadow Sonnet

After viewing Anila Quayyum Agha's
installation, *Intersections,* Rice Gallery, Houston
Vanessa Zimmer-Powell

I know the shadows of oak; at this hour
they trace their lace on the homeless body
at the edge of campus, on the students
who need the calm of shade sometimes, and then
there's me, the interloper, collecting
intersections formed by absence of light,
frottages that linger like dark henna,
or a smell that I carry when I leave
the presence of a stranger. She was
breathing into a respirator and smelled
like orange Ivory, if that exists, you know
I carry her into traffic, the patterns of truck
shadows, a freeway where we do not move.
Each car spreads its gaunt halo of anger

or light.

Luminaria on Wellesley Drive: Albuquerque, 1978

one for Judith L. Florence

Eric Paul Shaffer

When the luminaria were lit, the eve began, the dark part
    at least, beneath stars and stubborn illumination

from the night. Luna was in the sky, a bright face glum
with reflections of the luminous eclipsed by the turning
of the world. On the sidewalk were brown paper sacks

bottomed with river sand from the south valley, burning
    candles within casting a glow of gold on snow,
while the light of the stars looks electric, cold and chaotic.

    Every last breath drifts into blue, deep and sparked
with old light. If the night were mine, I'd carry the title
to darkness with my hands in my pockets, but my fists

are knotted on nothing, and the sky lifts my eyes to look
    through the clouds from my mouth and see the cold,
universal turning that will end the eve, the winter, the world.

All I know is love dies as every voice and vision passes,
and days grow lighter or darker as seasons come and go,
and since I know that, I know all will end, even eventually

me. The street is empty with moon and candles and snow
and stars, and with all that light, there's nothing I can't see.

Lisa P. Thomas, **Southwest Perspective**

The Evolution of Light

Carol Barrett

First the air clears
its palette, exaggerates
the light: what was burnt

sienna, now sleek maroon
foothills. What was green,
blurred commotion of field, boy

and dog. Ahead the sky
splinters and light
rains down. Will we make

the dousing we came for --
twigs bent to the source --
or miss this manifestation,

arrive in the aftermath,
flood and stone, stories
already gathering?

Drops begin, the splashing light,
now a dozen three-toed woodpeckers
on the roof. Is the drumming

fastest where, but for the veil
of cloud, we no longer see?
Or here, sky drenching us

indigo? Isn't it always
so: future bursting over
the pueblo that lies, perhaps,
in sunlight, just ahead.
A remote telephone wire
and a single crow
about to be joined:
the only way
to prepare for the rapture
is to lift the feet lightly.

Haunting Old Neighborhoods

Paul Christensen

You grew up here, in the soot
of an iron mill, the blackened
doorways of a slaughter house.
A sky the color of steel
welds the cemetery to the horizon.
The planet is drunk and whirls
its way behind a weary sun,
kicking the moon into a pit of stars.

Clothes hung from your
narrow shoulders, your scrawny hips.
You used to dance your way home
from school, book bag for a tambourine.
Your mouth as red as a gypsy's
with the sucker balls you rolled
across your tongue. Your eyes closed
for lack of wanting anything.

Love was not yet walking by herself,
but toddling from couch to chair,
crying gibberish that could have been
your name, your destiny.
All that's behind you now.
Standing on your shadow, you wonder
what made all this so beautiful
it stabbed you in the heart.

Pacifica

Bernard Briggs

You'd be forgiven for thinking
that sharing the same name
as your neighbour, meant you were related.
If not now, then sometime in the past.
Maybe you could knock on their door
meet up and have a beer
become friends for life.
Enjoy the views together
check out family memories
with old photos of a younger you.
Swap stories by the fireside
even exchange a gift of two.

What you wouldn't expect is that
they'd start stealing your land
one piece at a time. Your garden
a tumble of sandstone here.
Your living room wall
a nibble of concrete there.
Your furniture, family heirlooms
splinters of wood and glass
falling into their clutches.
You'd probably move away
wouldn't you, after all
possession is nine tenths of the law
or ten tenths, if it's waving goodbye.

Old Creek Barn

to Giana Gray
Luke J. Johnson

My daughter doesn't smell the mold, the dog dander—
wood rot wilting in a truck's rusty ribs.

She doesn't see maws
from termites,

places where rats
shit into splinters   left nests
buried under saw blades.

Mustard murmurs
as far as she can see,

and beyond that: timberline
tucked in the sky's gun metal gauze,

and beyond that: the Pacific
glittering like topaz—
white wash whisked inside a breeze.

I want so badly to inform her
that this place is more
metamorphic for death—a Dali Painting—

than it is dance: something transcendent,
or life-affirming.

But before I can consider
my fatherly angle—my proverbial advice—

she's moved on
to the music of water   slipping
by stones.

Abandoned House, Placitas

Jan Selving

Give it a stash of buttons
and insect husks,
a slick hand sliding down
a shower stall, pipes
droning through
plaster walls. Give it
warmth,
      ballast,
more than this desert
lot by the interstate
where it sits on cinder
blocks like an elephant
on a drum, exposed
as an extracted tooth,
waiting for the owner
to return. I recognize it
from its old address,
one house among many
on a block of modest houses
built during the boom
after WWII. Good place
to raise a family—good
schools, a hospital nearby.
Out back a massive climbing

rose, out front the overgrown
root-buckled driveway.
And the garden—
a marvel of engineering—
terraced hillside, dirt
anchored by a farthingale
of soaker hoses.
Scavengers have taken
the hinges, knobs, copper
flashing, tile, molding sinks,
and floorboards.
A stripped doorway has
the puzzled glare of a face
without eyebrows.
Give it back a way
to lock itself up, blooms
raking a window.
Give it shutters.

Give sails to the two-story
hull run aground.

Bees have found
the ductwork, filled
the house with thrumming.
Spiders, flickers, mice
claim lathing and roof
beam. Dust falls over all
the food chains, oblivious
to us as a fossil to a footstep.
A breeze lifts a web—
nothing in mind. Beyond

the porch broken shell
gleams from the vast
once-ocean bed.

Wooden Overcoat

Erin Elkins Radcliffe

The body of a brown owl
ground down into tar—

feathers pointing up.
Three days pass:
not a single person will pick him up,

one jackknifed wing flapping
with each lowering of the wind.

○

A family lowers
a calf-sized box into the ground:

a shallow hole
cornered from the awful soil,

dry and flaked as a stack of old books.
A stooped gospel sharp

says the words, makes the signs—
damp at the only woman's eyes.

Someone managed a cross:
barbwire adjoining

a saguaro spine
split in two.

A dutiful tap-tap
of spine into earth:

the family and preacher depart.
The child's body settles,

snug in flannel and rildy,
as a fox turns around in its den.

Silent bats angle overhead,
dipping their faces

into saguaro flowers
that push their petals out past

the clinging, old light of the moon.

Noon Whistle, Electra

Susan Rooke

You never saw the town at night.
For all you knew it closed, deserted streets
cleared of the suspension-shot sedans
and rattling pickups, their mufflers growling
deep from the storm cellars of the underworld.
Storefronts might leak a deceptive blue glow,
but at the vacant fairgrounds, loudspeakers
in the rodeo arena would call out only
to the wind. In that sweat stain on the road
to Wichita Falls, named for some long-dead
rancher's daughter, city sophistication,
its ways with darkness, held no appeal.
Folks were too bedeviled by the light.
To steer them through their lives they had
the noon whistle, a siren that wailed of torment
and despair, so long and loud that farmers
in their fields could hear—abandoning tools,
tractors, chores—making for the dim indoors
where their iron-jawed wives perspired, waiting
with the midday meal. Because the sun's torch
blazed overhead even on a clouded day, even
in winter, and would brand the stooped shadow
of a man's shoulders on the earth.

Hearing the siren once was enough to tell you
that the anguished roar of it was a judgment
on your life, your shameful shiftless habits, that
you could never live there, and if you stayed
one moment longer that sound would be

the last thing you'd hear as your blood turned
to sludge, your tongue to dust in your mouth.

Thank God you were only passing through.

White Oaks

Dale Ritterbusch

He has a miner's hands,
fingers bent, broken, never set,
skin callused, stretched to breaking
over knuckles forced into a permanent fist.
His brow burns darker than desert rock,
deep canyons carved above his leathery eye.
His hair like mangled sinews
dried in the long drought sun
tangles in his cracked lips,
catches in his uncut nails.

Saying nothing,
he motions everyone away
with a contemptuous wave of his hand.

I suppose the desert could do this
to a sane man too,
but one who had forsaken all
for a woman who promised
against all reason she would come,
who built a home so many years before of stone,
where there was no stone, with a well,
where there was no water so much of the time,
who believed in the resurrection
of his spirit mingled with the spirit of that woman
who foretold all in late summer dreams

as a cool light crept beneath her clinging gown
and entered her, touching her breast
in wild, unfamiliar ways—
certainly, the desert
could do this to any man.

In its Victorian splendor his house still stands,
miles, decades, away: the nearest road
washed out quite long ago, the weather vane,
the windmill, rusted permanently into place;
and every crack that opens in the calcined sun
offers shelter for the lizards of his smile—
unconcerned and cold as the adobe past.

Christopher Woods, **Miner's Homes**

Slicing Pieces of the Ice

Alan Birkelbach

He would shovel snow for her
although no one could ever say he loved her.

When the icicles were thick,
hanging from her eaves

there in her New Mexico cabin
he would show up with a hack saw.

I mean thick ice, like inches thick,
medieval legendary dagger-thick.

He would saw an icicle right off the house
and, without a word, knock on her door,

and show her, still without a word,
the way the light would prism, indigo, violet,

through the cut clear root.
And he'd hand it to her and walk off her frozen porch

like a silent suitor delivering flowers.
A man might imagine he might have loved her once,

once upon a time, if they had lived in a warmer place.
But here he only had a shovel, a hack saw.

And lots of snow. And ice. No daffodils.
Nothing except blinding light that always made him squint.

Ghost Town

Pamela Ahlen

Imagine last chance,
imagine nothing left to lose,
men like tumbled weeds
blown by furnace winds,
funambulists on tight wires of prospect
come to quench adrenal rush,
folly soon enough gone bust —
towns named broken hills
and sulphur springs
rising like hot air balloons:
bank church jail saloon,
boneyard of iron filigree—
rough-toothed bowls of grit
forged with not a little calamity,
timber blast and muck
now heaves of dust
beneath bottle shards
and tin can sand, where
snakes sleep out the scorch—
and you're here
gulping for heat's relief—
and can't you feel them wandering,
flapping arms to wind,
souls berserk for holy gold?

Overtaken by a stampede of tumbleweed

Sheila Sanderson

on the wide plain of the Rio Puerco,
you remind yourself
that despite their acrobatics,
the excellent show
of gaining time and ground,
being of single mind
and purpose,
it's naught but the wind
busy rearranging the scenery.
You haven't much mind
or giddyup
for any business which can't be
conducted on the meander,
any that isn't throwing
buffalo gourds at stratocumuli
or picking up shards
of a home industry
now defunct.
They're warm as biscuits
from a day on desert hardpan.
Meanwhile the tumbleweeds
keep somersaulting
toward town.

Meanwhile your shirt-back dries
with a satisfying billow
and snap.
The sand stirs
into a slight scouring
of the backs of your legs.
Though you, too,
are a minion of the wind,
that's about all
the wind can do for you.

First published in *Keeping Even* (Stephen F. Austin University Press, 2012)

The Garnet Moon

Paul Zarzyski

After forking alfalfa to the horses,
you sit with your first cup,
first Tesuque sun easing through
windows in LaBajada red
adobe—like liquid tinted pink,
this cornsilk light runneling over the gentle-
curved sills. You feather
the long fingernail file
through beveled arcs and strokes, deliberate
as the violinist guides the bow. Your hands
cast shadows of dancers
to the flagstone floor—shadowed steam
from your coffee, a gossamer
curtain they make love behind
in a spirit breeze. Could this be
the kachina's silhouette—the sacred omen
we've craved in our lone quests
for the dance perfected?
                              I watch your fingers
whisking alfalfa leaf
from your gold hair, Zia sun
steepening into the room. This afternoon,
in blue sage and cholla along the Rio Grande,

we'll muse over a red ant hill,
smooth as workings of a jeweled watch.
You'll spoon, with the nail of your little finger,
a garnet they've mined
and maneuvered to their granular roof
shingled in glitter—a lone moon you'll choose
from this universe. As you lift it
slowly toward the palm I hold above the hill,
spill it and with your nail tip
roll it across the synapse
of all my nerves, a frenzy of ants
comes to a standstill
in this eclipse of lovers locked perfect for the dance.

For Elizabeth Dear

from *Wolf Tracks On The Welcome Mat*—Oreanabooks, 2003

Horse Love

karla k. morton

All day long, I've followed you on these
Denton County plains, wild Mexican
Mustangs, small and tough, just thirteen

hands high -- horseflesh more precious
than gold. It's a love affair as deep as
Texas -- a man and his horse.

I startle you and you run, the smell of white skin
new to your flaring nose. I stalk you weeks
at a time, until you linger, head down, as I near --

a beast smart enough to eye cracked soil, smell
burrowed creatures -- navigate holes just
waiting to break a stallion's leg; a rider's neck.

You are wind and fire and power and life.
Together we will chase our enemies,
tend our neighbours; draw thick wooden plows

deep in the earth. Some call it breaking -- to hunt
and corral and saddle and ride...but ours is a trust,
for on the edge of the chasm, or pot-holed plains,

or within the swelling creek bed, I am the one
on *your* back; you *choose* to carry me,
my faith as strong as the iron of your shoes.

Silver Terrace Cemeteries

Milla van der Have

Some mornings they come, the horses
wild beyond their years. You watch
them climb the hills, returning

to what once was ours: a simple stone
and miles of silver lining. After all,
time only folds in on itself, merely

curls its tail by way of warning.

You see them run that distant light,
ghosts of simple beck and call.
And for a single moment you remember

a sense of place: fleeting hooves
on deeper ground.

Portrait

Megan Merchant

Children fly black kites
across the dry lake bed,

their salt-white feet
float on the crust.

They laugh about
how they are ironing

the skin on their
abuela's face--

her ashed bones spread
years ago
in the veil of heat.

They mock the wind—
a single note

scolding them
with a wooden spoon
for dragging in such dust.

When the sun
bends, dissolves the

dust-stained light
they tuck themselves
into the cracks

and read the book
of the forgotten river,

the pages baked
into crow's feet
and laugh lines

around their abuela's
mischievous eyes.

Her lover, the coyote,
who swallowed
saguaro spines,

and hair grew more
bristled than soft,

howls at the iris
blinking

behind the quilt-edged
clouds
she neatens
into the corners
of sky.

Voodoo Spoons

Naomi Shihab Nye

When her father the old man died
 I was called to witness, to say
Yes, he really seems dead and knew
 we were entering another phase.

No more would he raise his hand to me
from the porch across the park.
No more ask what I knew, beg for a kiss,
where was I going, thank me for pie.

Now I had to hide from his daughter
whenever she came dragging a branch
or box down the sidewalk,
orange scarf tied under her chin.

The way she screamed my name
like a horror movie.
Had to dash through my door
as if I hadn't heard, otherwise

thirty minutes of mad chat -
not one scrap of sense – would ensue.
But I couldn't stop leaving things on her porch,
as I had done with her father for years…

never guessing she would think
they came from a spirit on the other side,
a hawk, or a bat. Antique spoons in a bundle,
nubbly vintage suit with golden buttons,

 holy card with glowing heart of wings.
He'd always known this meant, *I'm thinking of you.*
She thought – *they're watching, I'm circled by eyes,*
if I don't drink pomegranate juice, I'm doomed.

Father

David J. Bauman

He was born before spring, on the third day
of the third month of 1933, the year they laid
concrete on Hoover Dam. I'll never know
how he grew, slab by slab, the cold

copper veins the gradual hardening, the dark
tunnels of blood-boiling heat and poison gas,
the tense diversion of nature's power, rushing
youth, and the life his parents built on sacrifice

and solid ground. By the time I had arrived
he was tall and solid, with a deep canyon-voice,
he kept in reserve, as behind a stone, a wall
of power, sustaining, intimidating and resolute.

Only now do I begin to know
the vast calm beauty, deep as the Meade,
that rests behind the man, and begin
to fathom what it takes to tame a wild thing.

Clinging Peach

J. Scott Brownlee

My father holds the fruit up to my face, saying, "Here, son—
smell this." It's a pink peach as ripe as my life used to be

before smoking & gin. He's a careful man, sober & awkward
in public, though friendly to strangers in conversation.

Once at a Houston Astros game he met a snuff-dipping cowboy
who gave us tickets at the gate as an act of kindness: bullpen seats

near the edge of the field where we dreamed I'd play ball in The Bigs
as a gifted lefty. I broke my father's foot instead pitching sliders to him

from the mound in high school. He shared this fact with me years afterward.
Incredulous at first, laughing, I could not believe it. After the stroke

he forgets things sometimes—but not box scores, or peaches,
or chicken-fried feasts. He loves Hoover's, a "down-home" restaurant

in the heart of Austin. He's a decent man. Most of my life I have tried
& failed not to be him, treating my girlfriends with respect even when

they leave me due to disagreements. "Never date twins," he told me
while we ate dinner. His crooked smile gave the path of his own past away

as he chewed his cobbler. "Sometimes wrong turns feel right," he said.
"Make some. Trust me." When I smell peaches on the street headed out

to the store for some small nourishment, when I go on a date with the decent
woman who will offer to split the check, kiss me slowly, let me lie in her bed

& not shoot heroin, argue blindly, or cheat, I remember his words & am thankful
for them, their consistency unlike the changeable world's. When I make love's

mistake for the last time—the one in which clinging becomes certain, necessary—
I will break down completely & know I love her without second guessing.

I will mean it, say it with the confidence my father tried to teach me
stating simply, "I've missed you," with blunt honesty nights he came home

from work as a twice-failed lawyer. "You're my Air Wolf," he'd say.
"You're my helicopter." Then the spinning, the falling back slowly to earth

where he put me down gently, then, as anything. The lithe woman I need
will feel similarly when I twirl her body in the distant future confirming

that she does not, in fact, have a twin as I tell her the story of when permanence
took root, entering us—how my father advised strongly I marry her

the first night we went out to eat "for questioning," & she treated
his broken-down lawyer antics with the same excitement as I did

while spinning, making me feel that night a surreal certainty, all that
came after it in a shining instant as inevitable as each limb on each tree

in our backyard orchard. "Branched between us there may be, *perhaps* be,
with luck," I'll say kneeling to lift her, "spring peaches clinging."

Teaching the Silence to Hurt

Ciara Shuttleworth

I guess if you see your dad get arrested
often enough, you don't get embarrassed about anything
don't want him back
to do the job you're doing better.

Until Frank's dad never came back
and his mom went

into the same bottles
his dad had smashed against
walls, the floor, her head.

Frank kept
the lawn and for weeks we stole pints of paint in our school bags for the house
so the neighbors watching through righteous squints could see
no reason to take him away, too.

    *

We lay on the kitchen floor,
let water run over
the sink edge—

our little waterfall—us below trying to drown
out his bad. Smoothed like river stones.

We thought we could put out all the fires,
the riotous windows of the street
finally judging us
   as children only,

but all we could do
was mop up,
take the bottle
from his mother's sleeping hand,

sit, wet, in the summer night
with the whiskey.

*

Frank drove a stolen sedan into the concrete
embankment under the overpass
I'd taken years before
      leaving town for good.

For days no one
thought to look, his mother
wandering the house in search of a bottle
before stumbling, cursing

damn in her bathrobe down
the street, the windows glimmering
with no one to help.

Breaking Ground

Jerry Bradley

Flat-chested as West Texas, the girls caravaned to the coliseum
to see Elvis, passing acres of chopped cotton and gas pumps
that stood like one-armed veterans a decade after the war.
Billboards hawked cheap rooms, tractors, used furniture,
but their engines purred like housecats all the way.

                         The moon
on the horizon was as ripe as a peach and just as full,
but even then it was old fashioned to rely on things you could see.
No longer ensorcelled by the browns surrounding them,
they sought transformation in omens from a rockabilly boy
with sideburns, and that night they stared at the truth
until they could no longer see:
                         the spectacle of a warmup trio
led by a boy with T. J. Eckleburg eyes, a rock-and-roll hammer
ready to break Lubbock's hardest heart.

                         Four years later
his plane and career were victims of hapless gravity.
The girls, long back in their homes, had turned boyfriends
into husbands and were already retelling old lies. What museum
records their sadness now? Beneath the billboards and floorboards,
who furrows their fields, the dirt that none of them could quite leave behind?

Silver Leaf

Kevin Marshall Chopson

I love the silver leaf of wind-blown trees
forced to show us their hidden side
as cloudy days roll back the green.

I love how the long, thin branches of mimosa
reach out to the road offering their pink hands
to strangers, and to me . . .

I'll drive south to smaller and smaller towns
where scarecrows gather in the dark, circle the fire,
and pray a spark doesn't catch.

I'll stand in rows of corn, a stalk in each hand,
and listen to their talk – language, smooth as silk,
spoken through mouths of bent straw . . .

Deeper in, and gone too far for a night like this,
I'll find the river's edge and float on truth to the other side,
set my feet down in the red mud of Oklahoma.

We Arrive at Three Rivers

Kyce Bello

The long drive from the malpais
left me thirsty,

but I didn't even whisper
into our silence.

That Tularosa country
is filled with brush, small

gray branches twisting along
the highway.

Every creekbed we crossed was dry,
but in the willow thickets

you found stone bottomed pools.
Waterbugs mated in eddies.

Cress greened the line
between land and stream.

I didn't know what you wanted,
but sat tending to the dust

on my hands and lips.
After bathing, we made a fire

of Algerita branches
and watched its flames,

those hidden waters
rustling at our backs.

San Juan Relief: Yellow Blooms
In Early March

Ken Hada

I'm a hundred miles down the road
from that one spot in the trout stream
where I stand transfixed, the water
hypnotizing me as I concentrate
on the fly and the hunted fish.

My only respite is to look up
resting my eyes on a low bluff
bordering the stream, covered
with sage grass in yellow bloom.

The rust-red rock, the dusty green
stems, sandy yellow flowers
in subtle relief, my eyes look up
to dull blue sky, charcoal clouds.

Two hundred, five hundred miles
down the road driving toward duty
that unnamed boulder endures
just above the water – flowers bloom
wild, yellow in early March.

Reaching Kanab

Travis Truax

The broken and varied
vermillion cliffs of southern Utah.
September— and I've been gone
two days. The dangerous dry
roads of red desert, blank and grey
beneath my car.

I can go 300 miles on one tank.

Abandonment is a common word
along hundreds of western roads.
And death, a common thought
in these red rock spaces.

My sorrow commits to vagrant
paths, desert tracks. An artist's
disappearance, Escalante Canyon,
1934.

It is the high desert hope
that things are remembered.

White

Jan Selving

The girl watches her father smoothly navigate
a switch-back mountain road,

windshield an Etch-a-Sketch, the coal
of his cigarette a stylus scoring a crazy

route along the glass, red trails lingering
in smoke. Inside the giant cave

his head scrapes the ceiling. He meters a stone
nest of ruin. Old fires blacken the ground.

He's un-phased by parallax, packed dirt floor
now ceiling, stone towers dangling

like stalactites within the ground glass.
The shutter wheezes, echoes from the giant

cave mouth as she walks ahead to the smaller
caves father up the trail. White elongations—

torsos—some species of spirit robot,
heads wired to the Mother Ship,

float on mottled of red ochre. Here and there
       spirals—stars, bursts of ether, time-lapsed

and buzzing a light she traces with her fingertip,
       borders between skin and etched stone

fusing along this ghost path's close concentric lines.
       White hands scatter like Styrofoam packing.

Palm to palm, she pushes one as if it were
       a latch. She can almost feel it giving way

into the cool other side, her hand the eclipse
       that opens.

Driving West

Jeanetta Calhoun Mish

East of I-35

. . . this melancholy of returning home to mountain New Mexico from Oklahoma heart-home. The further west, the more *cholla*-prickly, defensive, out of sorts Gulping last miles of thick water-air, ardently cataloguing cardinals, blue herons, scissortails. Summoning Okies I leave behind—artists, musicians, radicals, writers, outlaws, backwoods philosophers—lament catches in my throat and gut wrenches. Rivers and creeks run red, challenging cutbanks. Ditches deep as sorrow. Sapphire sky. Redbuds and dogwoods and wild plums; fence-row blackberries and delicate willows in early spring. Joy said: *Oklahoma will be the last song I ever sing.* My body harmonizes in minor key.

West of I-35

60+ miles on State Highways 11 & 64 running due west from Blackwell with single one-mile-north correction in respect of river. Paralleling the Mason-Dixon. My truck sandwiched between three drilling fluids tankers and a workover rig. New Holland disc harrows perch in fields, folded, like red mayflies. Miles and miles of turned earth; forgotten cemeteries mourning disappeared communities. Shotgunned historical marker: all that remains of Stella, Quaker settlement. Salt Fork of Arkansas River snakes back and forth under the highway. Marshes of Great Salt Plains lifting into air on wings of white-face ibis. Here: an Oklahoma seen once before from B&N freight-train caboose, Enid-Alva-Blackwell-Arkansas City. Small towns and cabooses: *Ubi Sunt?*

I-15: Introverts and Strangers on the Long-Range Shuttle

A story has to leave out nearly everything or nobody can follow it.

—Kate Greenstreet

Nano Taggart

Sandstone cliffs frame a cold day in March
on the other side of glass I press both hands against.

He begins, *Think about how much time these mountains—*
Christ, if you lived here all your life you're missing it.

Part of this now, struck by a response, I leave my safe
silence for, *we studied it in school—glaciers, fault lines,*

geologic time. But they may leave out that last bit now.
It's going to be a long day, I don't say it but think it.

(Nothing changes for this lack of offering.) —*Still,* his
fingers uncoil toward me, *revelry, they can't teach revelry.*

The landscape shifts from sedentary red to igneous black.
—*They can and they do, just not for these mountains.*

Two warm days preceded this one. Both hands balled now
under a folded jacket, my first memory has been solicited—

he's getting to something. I consent with, *I'm standing in*
Lake Mojave to my knees, couldn't have been more than three.

I don't request his, or note the photo of this moment, how
doubt clouds recollection: the sun in my eyes, my mother's

outstretched hand. We both suspect people gather to water
or to landmarks a safe distance from water. 200 miles closer

to a shared destination, I've reached an accord with a stranger.
It's never as simple as, *this sustains us, we should stay right here.*

Blues in Bisbee

John Lambremont, Sr.

Most of the musicians are grizzled veterans,
with years of riding the Southwest circuit
from Los Angeles to Lubbock and Abilene
and all the stops in between, save
the piano-pounding lady
that also wails on tenor sax
and the youthful Navajo power trio
whose blues-tinged psychedelia
a la Jimmy the Page
and Jimi the King,
wows the aging crowd.

Shade is in short supply,
and breezes are blessings,
as this heat is no longer dry,
even at a mountain altitude;
humidity is at an all-time high,
in the Rockies, Boulder is awash,
and it's cats and dogs in Albuquerque.

You find escape in a jungle gym's base,
a corner with shade and a good view of the stage,
and it's okay; most kids here are someone's grand-kids,
though they are few and far between,
and the swing and slide and monkey bars
are holding them in sway.

Bandanas out-number baseball caps,
and tattoos out-do fake boobs,
although both are in abundance.
Sixty is the new twenty-five,
as boomers and hippies that have survived
try to do their best with less
to keep their fading dreams alive.

Janis Joplin Buys Her First Record Albums

Susan J. Erickson

The wind is tied to a stake in this town. My foot
is caught in the same loop and I am thirsty

for the solace of rebellion. How much of life
can you see when the highest place in town

is a water tower? Getting high in this town
means walking to the top of the Rainbow Bridge—

high enough to let a Navy destroyer pass under.
When I climb onto the catwalk and let my legs

dangle and swing over the side, blue lights flash,
the police arrive. For God's sake, this is not

how I will leave town. At sea level my breath
escapes like car exhaust. The air smells of sulfur

and my skin is singed. I would go up in flames
without the albums of Leadbelly and Bessie Smith.

I hop the freight-train of their voices, ride someplace
where being me is a song not yet written.

Persistent Dream

(for Janet)

Peter Ludwin

Of all the shelters people contrive
for themselves on the border—
buses, yurts, trailers, caves,

the crumbling, reconstructed ruins—
your one-room *ranchera* house
was always my favorite.

The two stone columns Manuel built
in the grip of a cocaine habit
create illusion, like the desert itself

and the lives of people we knew.
Each winter when I arrived
from the north I marveled

at your lush vegetation: the outsized
greasewood, ocotillo that spiraled
like El Greco's figures toward God-drunk

reunion, the ghostly blue-gray *candelilla*.
Walking the shrine trails that wove
through that wild garden, I craved an Eden

of my own. Whenever a storm turned
the mountains dark, greasewood savaged
by wind, my roots grew ever more stubborn.

Until death emptied that house.
Until, after a raven flew down the arroyo,
the greasewood itself stopped waving.

Kathy Rudin, **Airstream, Marfa**

Elegy for Eric Moe

Matthew Dulany

We might have had someplace to go,
it might have been New Mexico,
and might have raced,

she and I, to clear the canyon
before the helicopter dropped the dynamite,
but we'd sort of cracked up

the pickup twice already, and possibly
were something like low on luck.
From the white mountainside white

rabbits leapt, multiplying massing,
to heap across the only road out –
like the future, higher than ourselves.

Then, awaiting excavation,
ruins in that house you made with your hands,
earthed in adobe, absorptive stone,

the windows framing southern summits
untouched, what a treat it was
to be avalanched-in with your sister.

Razing the Set

William Virgil Davis

In the end there is only the wind
and a few bushes blown through the scene.
The façade has been taken down
and carried off in trucks. The cast
has gone long ago. Even the few
extras, a stunt man or two,
several indiscriminate animals
used for background shots, are gone.
The wind picks up. The sand,
like a curtain let down,
covers everything. The place
will only exist if you insist on it.
Not even the night would remember.

Originally published in the *Three Rivers Poetry Journal*; it was
recently reprinted in *Dismantlements of Silence: Poems Selected and
New* (2015).

from **Let That Fire Catch Me Now**
Kevin Goodan

Sun purpled at its apex.
A strange wind twisting trees
Before they ignite, radiant heat
Killing the buckbrush, white berries
Bursting into char. This is now,
The journey in which nothing
Is auguried, and what is called fate
Resides in the aleatorics of flame.
Here is the language of incineration.
How far can a body run
When it's encased in fire?
How do we convey the transference
Into ash? To trap, to keep what is
Known to us? What do we do
When all the thousand hour fuels
Have ignited? When crews
Were finally able to recover
The bodies, they found the fingers
In each gloved hand were broken.

*   *   *

We station ourselves along the slope.
We've calculated windshift,
The fire's own need for air.
When the radios click we uncap
Our flare and strike them,
Breathing in sulfuric puffs
As the neon flames spurt
To the thick brush we light
Making a fire that marries fire
And halts it. We daub our flares
Here and there, scribe intentions
On the dark where every move
Becomes a function of light,
A cursive that whispers our names
To the overstory as we double-click
Our mics, strapped to our chests
Like crucifixes that guide us
Through the night-burn, back
Into our dreams once more.

Flame, Perhaps

Jerry Craven

Beside a green and dying river, new
California flame breaks among leaves
reduced to yellow dry kindling catching
sparks from an almost defeated fire.

I have long lived on an edge of heat,
from a moist-wet first wail in Doctor
White's South Texas clinic to a hot
September Angelina forest safe
today from hungry Western wildfires.

Wandering between Amarillo winter
frozen waters and burning California
are decades of edges, warm and cool, wedding
and death, my father handing me a cane pole
for hot bayou summers, my mother placing
hundred dollar bills behind light switch
plates as her final winter approached;
my teenage first love Sara with heaving
breast and lips in hot passion, then Sara
saying farewell with an indifferent nod to vanish
into those decades, then Sara struck into icy
death by her very breasts; handing my son
a cane pole beside Lake Meredith
waters warm, seeing his pale face
through cold iron bars locked by his burning

pipe and hot needles; my own panting
races on legs now holding me
cold on a colder edge the very day
of that flowing green river between
ashen earth and yellow leaves aflame,
perhaps both awaiting judgment, and perhaps
I choose the river. Or that flame, perhaps.

Fabrice Poussin, **Lost in the Desert**

The Spark

Charles A. Stone

In West Texas the bare bones of day
Struggle with parched deserts
To see how long life remains
Upright in the hands of heat
So intense it bends the spines
Of mountains

Here and there a cross of naked trees
Twists in the dust of river beds
And prickly pear cactus stand
Stalwart as needles drop
From scorched pads

Even sound is blistered here
and collapses to the wayside
where no one hears its bones
crack or the creak of spines
as trees scratch the flats
for water

When the world catches fire
the spark could well launch
itself from West Texas
where even rain is fire
and rocks burn.

Ice Storm, November 2015

Steven Schroeder

Ice has the world dreaming
fire. A glaze of hard light
numbs eyes into thinking
white everywhere. But it is

nothing of the kind.
Red earth pales, drifting
down the face of a long plateau
while yellow grass lies low,

bends to white but does not
break. Trees kneel until they
give way to endless prairie.

Windmills tall as a city rise, dissolve
in ghostly light, one in three
blades visible. Nothing moves.

Trail Marker

Allyson Whipple

A trail not big enough
for two abreast – my lover
has short legs, walks
behind me. She keeps
her eyes trained on
the trickle of river, listens
for the drying waterfalls.
How is her body thriving
in the heat, after all the fire
we made? My skin thins
in the sun.

She isn't just
olive; she's ale, red wine,
caramel. She is dessert,
and I've been fasting.

But this can't survive
the desert. This can't
survive drives of
two hundred miles
for momentary closeness.

This doesn't stop her lips
from marking mine.
That doesn't stop her sweat
from turning to perfume.
That doesn't stop me
from noticing the younger,
harder bodies here,
and turning – and turning
my head back toward her.

Nevertheless New West True Gospel

JV Brummels

Imagine there's no heaven . . . .

Simple man past pride
school-teacher poor
up and over from the plains
on the backside of the front range
where money ain't nothing
but derivatives and change
I watch through this Saturday
this brand-new town
slithering across the valley floor

Enough to make eagles cry
I'm slaking my thirst
and my first
      legal Rocky Mountain high
in the Dusty Boot brewpub
among pioneer families
of accountants
      in madras sports shirts
short pants and flipflops
their tired women
      hair rinsed to faded gingham
pacifying the teething babies
      cranky in their laps

What a fool I look –
circuit-rider black hat
feet scuffed in authentic dirt
square on my round ass
like a kid mowing the lawn
        in crash helmet and pads
solitary behind bistro glass
studying Founders Avenue
a wide-angle view of a town
glittering in the sun like bricks
        of plastic-wrapped bank notes

the oldest monumental stack –
Established 2006 –
fronted by a bronze plaque
partnering the names
of the three rich and lucky
        hard-rock sons of bitches
who prospected this mother lode
        out of high thin air

What a failure I am
not to have struck here first
to speak only the language
of one lonely tribe
        among this earth's citizens

I lift my stare past the marquee
of summer sci fi blockbusters
and the manufactured Italian place
      for the long view –
concentric rings of houses
      like brightly painted circled wagons
At least no steeples scratch
at the peace of the peaks

My business here's simple as ever
the oldest of professions –
trading grass for flesh
      flesh for grass –
between scrabbling out some few truths
amid the graves of many others
      buried bodies along the back trail
my only rule
      to break at least one rule
Beyond that I don't know what to do
but wave over the tab
leave green currency among plastic cash

Outside three tense deputies
study the façade of my fresh smile
as if this late in geologic time
any of us could do
      a damn thing about it

The Strait of Magellan
   (for Tracy)
         Peter Ludwin

You did all those wild and crazy things
most people only dream about, and the rest
slump at their desk. When you moved to the desert

you lived for a month in a cave and hiked naked
through the Mexican outback, rappelling down cliffs
with tourists so blown out their shit took flight like owls.

One night a voice commanded you to go to the Strait of Magellan.
You called your father and told him you'd been summoned
to the end of the world. You could hear him shatter,

but when he collected himself he bought you a ticket
to Chile. And you flew, hitched and rode
until you arrived where rock dove under the sea.

You tell me you're hard to get to know. I understand
why you say it. It's true because, as you say also,
you'd rather get in trouble once in awhile

than be mediocre. You've worn the stinging nettle
like a collar, received what you wished for.
That's why you haven't been hard to know at all.

Two weeks of learning Spanish from Carlos
on the fly, storms external, internal,
long nights coked out in Bolivia:

among even such thorns as these a certain compassion
settled in, infused the storyteller with no clothes
left to hide behind, no envelope left to push.

Have you noticed that here, in the lush profusion
of a garden hacked from the unforgiving desert,
there is water, water everywhere?

El Rey

Michael Thompson

Every town in the southwest
has an El Rey Motel
and none of them
is up to any good

Dead bugs in the window sill,
an AC unit that barely works
and three functional channels
are the mandatory staples

You can count on someone screaming
in the room next door
for no good reason

Rug burns are worn with regularity
by those who can't turn
a blind eye to the wreckage
from a bed of fire

Strangers have been known
to commit suicide there
when nothing goes as planned

It wouldn't catch me off-guard
if I woke up in between
Lydia Lunch and Exene Cervenka
with my jugular vein exposed
and dried blood around their mouths.

Fabrice Poussin, **Alamogordo, New Mexico**

Another Night at the Maverick Inn

Scott Wiggerman

I can no longer tell whether they're
arguing or fucking or both,
their earth-thirsty interludes
of growls and grunts and slurs
battering the wall between our rooms.
Better, I guess, than guests
with blaring infomercials or insipid
laugh tracks, but I want to sleep.
Why can't motel walls
be insulated enough to avoid
every sudsy stream of piss,
every thrusting headboard bang?
Are these walls made of the same
toilet paper I've been hearing
roll off its spindle each night
at one a.m., and again at four?
I've got the AC cranked,
the squeaky ceiling fan whirring,
but nothing's loud enough
to drown out the randy—or angry—
couple, except when the train
thunders by, shrieking,
the conductor's sadism let loose.
Of course, the drapes don't close
entirely on either of the windows,
the sink has a continual drip,
and the pillows are lumpy
as biscuits and country gravy—
much that same gray color too.

Yet when I visit Alpine,
there's no other place
I'd rather stay. The truth is,
I don't sleep much better at home.

A Casual Glance

David Thomas

A woman comes
    into this old barroom
from time to time
        when I'm lucky
         to be here
           too
slender
for Reubens
but just as round as he
    liked to paint
the women
he chose to celebrate
    I admire
    her proportions
an exquisite bloom
    of flesh
her face
might be thought plain
    but Modigliani
would see beauty
in the planes
    of those cheeks

and the startling
       intelligence
              of her eyes
as she absorbs my
       admiration
whether she wants it
          or not.

Happy Hour, Tucson

Charles Thielman

The deep blue flags of dusk unfurl
above happy hour at the Sidecar,

bar mirror catching
the eyes ready

to spout embers, the eyes
extinguishing flares.

This factory worker tossing back
the grease of cheap whiskey,

pumping work-born pains
into marrow. Worn hands

wrapped around bottle necks,
glasses, releasing cargoes,

juke box singer leaving
his heart on a hill.

The Seventh Wave

Red Shuttleworth

Hankering of the brain… in waves…
oxygen-rich or oxygen-starved blood.
Like beautiful, plucky coyote girls
from beneath a dappled moon.

Or like a loud yellow GMC pick-up crumpling-
bloody a couple of maimed, skin-tumored,
exhausted old miners… on Idaho Street in Elko.

A skinny waitress at Stockman's
is coming down, way down, surfing down
off something; cracked lips, big shiny hair,
side-mouth spittle, a busted heart
lugged too many goddamned miles.

What about your fever-slippery dream
during a TV blast of Redford in *Electric Horseman*?

Sonofabitch…. Falls out of a fake leather
arm chair at the Thunderbird Motel,
spills his drink, tries to ignore
his saggy neck skin image in the mirror,
clutches a greasy skunk hide leg blanket.

No... You're slammed by some seventh wave
in your brain central sulcus or precentral gyrus!
Drunken excess: *I been in five cinder block motels*
this past week... mistakin' my identity.

Hankerings on the brain: pipe-rattlin' motel,
half-dead eyes with black plastic sheets
nailed up from inside to doze a few hours
after driving mean, hard, n' restless
all the way from knobby Utah... other motels
that smell of cigarettes 'n feedlot...
of scamp-around girls who joy-jabber
about first sex in one-horse trailers.

You can't get a baggie to go, the waitress says,
or I can pour iced tea on your chicken fried steak.
She snaky-walks, loves *agricultural product.*
She's got a twang-radio mouth, sips bourbon
from a bogus-silver Doc Holliday flask.

Your brain doesn't rightly know if it's riding
wild-high tide or scraping bottom rock.

First published in *The Seventh Wave* chapbook. Bunchgrass Press,
Columbia Basin, Washington (2011, 2015)

For the Sad Waitress at the Diner in Barstow

Alexis Rhone Fancher

beyond the kitchen's swinging door,
beyond the order wheel and the pass-through piled
high with bacon, hash browns, biscuits and gravy,

past the radio, tuned to 101.5-FM
All Country - All the Time,
past the truckers overwhelming the counter,
all grab-ass and longing.

in the middle of morning rush you'll
catch her, in a wilted pink uniform,
coffee pot fused in her grip, staring over
the top of your head

you'll follow her gaze, out the fly-specked, plate
glass windows, past the parking lot,

watch as she eyes those 16-wheelers barreling
down the highway, their mud guards
adorned with chrome silhouettes of naked women
who look nothing like her.

the cruel sun throws her inertia in her face.
this is what regret looks like.

maybe she's searching for that hot day in August
when she first walked away from you.

there's a choking sound
a semi makes, when it pulls off the
highway; that downshift a death rattle
she's never gotten used to.

maybe she's looking for a way back.
maybe she's ready to come home.

(But for now) she's lost herself
between the register and the door, the endless
business from table to kitchen, she's

as much leftover as those sunny side eggs,
yolks hardening on your plate.

Prescilianos Café: Cuba, New Mexico

Ken Hada

It's not a morning for talking
only two others in the café.

I whisper my order – burrito
with green chili. She pours
coffee with a faint smile
no flirting, no banter.

It's quiet, like the valley
beneath the green mountains
under crystal sky.

She's diligent –
mixed-race, fair skin, hazel eyes,
canyon-blonde hair.

She wears long red earrings,
a white ruffled top,
black nylon pants, sandals

and when she speaks
her accent gently clinks
against my ear like ice
in a glass of summer tea

no ring on her finger
no cross on her neck.

Driving from Bloomfield
south on 550 through
remote landscape dotted
with yellow-tipped cholla

broomweed, juniper, dusty
mesas in the distance,
ochre and broad against
blue sky and puffy clouds

you feel the descent
into this sleepy village
shaded by mountains.

It's time for breakfast
time to sit quietly
in a vinyl booth
notice wood beams above

sip coffee and remember
the trout you caught
the osprey overhead
while you stood numb
in clear cold water.

Take another sip, feel
the sadness in her eyes
beyond the smile.

Lean back, stretch
stream-weary legs, think
about the long road home.

Coffee Café Blues (San Marcos, TX)

Bradley R. Strahan

The music is mournful-modern,
just what students want.
The "Barista" is cute, much too
for an *old gray* like you,
who still feels, somewhere
in his deepest delusions,
that he's still 39.
Well, even then,
you were too old for her.
Ah, but you still recall
those women who looked
hardly older & yet loved you
back in your *fabulous 40s.*

Why should anyone care?
It was the usual *wine and roses*
for a year or four, then no more.
Well, re-up my cup kid
and I'll sit & stare out
at another Texas town square,
complete with courthouse & cowboy.

Don't ask why I'm here,
wasting away, waiting
for a mistimed meeting,
while the parade of bikes & pick-ups
passes and my java gets as cold
as my jive. Why play poet?
Hey, the Bard said it's all a play.
So, *If my blues don't get you*
well my poems surely will.

The crew sleeps, snores, scattered
like an alien constellation in the sky.
Even the stars are hazed with dust
and smoke from burned out fires.

High Desert Arizona

Sheila Sanderson

Like an old-timer
easy with hard luck
will roll up pantleg
and shirtsleeve
to show what
a snapped cable
or a black widow
can do,
the land here
bares its stories
about where wind
makes its rounds
on rock,
has taught ridgeline
junipers to twist;
about where water goes
by habit
and by fancy,
where water went
and changed
its mind,
where a scrub oak
wanted so bad
for water,
it lay down on
its side and
cracked granite
to have it.

First published in *Southern Poetry Review* and *Keeping Even* (Stephen F. Austin University Press, 2012)

Tucson, 1968

Doug Anderson

We were still, I think, beautiful,
even after that jug of cheap Chianti
that stained her teeth and t-shirt,
our breath combined enough to kill
an orchid. I watched her sleep.
Air thick with orange blossoms
and morning light pinged the Catalinas
like a tuning fork, awake.
Now back to her and tangle legs,
warm in the yet cool spring.
She not quite awake,
answered back with arms.
An hour or two, and then at it again,
once more before coffee,
and sorely we untangled for the day.

Cortez

Steve Myers

She looked sinuous, wind-sculpted, fourteen at best.
How she'd made hotel desk receptionist
when she might have been out with those we'd seen
herding toddlers in front of battered trailers,
or on corners peddling dreamcatchers,
was another mystery of high-desert
America—the vanished Anasazi,
the Seven Cities...She'd only half-mastered
what her boss had taught her: nails hard-lacquered
orange, the color of globe mallow petals,
but bitten to the quick, a grown-up black shift
down the schoolgirl body to the bare
left foot that twisted inward, as if from shyness,
though it wasn't that—she limped badly, a foal
doubled-hobbled. When I asked the best route
to Santa Fe she said *I've never been,*
but I know what you mean. It first sounded
ditzy, then empty only as the wind
is empty in the ancient stories,
soughing ceaseless through boughs of piñon pines.

Leaving Las Vegas

David Olsen

Alluringly slim in slit skirt
and confident in the samba
of her walk, this willowy

chanteuse from Ipanema waits
in a desert of ochre and sage
with a battered leather case

holding everything she owns,
save the gestating remembrance
of that smooth blackjack dealer.

She could face a defeated return
to the roadhouse in Victorville,
but for now she has her looks.

Jaunty and defiant in stance,
she watches the onrushing dust
stirred by a new Cadillac.

She's ready for whoever comes.

Coyotes

Adrian C. Louis

On a stark, sandy hill
two coyotes danced
furry ear to furry ear,
attempting the tango
in timid moonlight.

Seated at the kitchen table
two hours later, they both
began to howl over some
minor calamity, some
failed disambiguation,
but soon they blubbered
& came to their senses
in a calm recollection
of their dance & the moon
& the fact that they would
never even consider ripping
each other's furry throats
if they gave up the bottle.

Kathy Rudin, **Abandoned Cabin, Marfa**

My Face is Scary but I am a Cowboy I Promise I'm Here to Help

Alex Lemon

If you are dumb
Is it really my duty
To explain it all
To you? Please, do
Not forget to chew
Before you swallow.
If you chew, spit
Now & again. That's
Almost all the lead
I got in this
Pencil. Remember:
The lead I got
In this pencil.
Remember:
History's hung
Droop & swing
Down from
The sky & this
Is what is called
Most commonly
Your shadow.
Dry wash, gulley,
A cactus that
Never blooms.
Apparitions
Cut the day into
A delicateness

We fail to
Comprehend.
I'm ready to be
Done with this
Drought, the endless
Brands on my
Back that boil
Hotter at night.
I'm going to
Leave my finger-
Guns right here
By the sink, floating
In this pickling
Jar—pigs' feet,
The wrinkled
Ears of my foes—
While I go stir
The frying okra
With my tongue.

Scorpion Mezcal

Catfish McDaris

He ate tortillas dipped in honey
then rode an owl across the
windy Guadalupe Mountains

Possum Sabbath was playing
in a cantina, Quick ordered a
double mezcal with a scorpion
in the bottle ready to strike

The barkeep said, "We don't
carry that poison anymore, it
made my pet coyote go blind"

Quick jerked his hog leg and
laid it on the bar, "Give me
some Zapotec juice from
Monte Alban before I do
something you'll regret"

The band started playing Little
Feat, Quick danced with a pretty
senorita, then they went outside
and jumped into the river of love.

East Cevallos Street

James H. Duncan

after dusk standing outside the patio cantina
and a train of boxcars crawls through

clouded night sky a ghostly reflection
of the cantina's carnival lights

waiting in line with those hoping to receive
holy communion with the night gods

counter girls hand out beers and couples
watch the train struggle along inches at a time

drinking the holy water of the night gods
for reverie, the numbing of our universal pain

the train of boxcars calls out, clatters and whines,
a church on rails moving south and westward

beer in green bottles, beer in brown bottles
saints & saviors, rusted & singing

while desire rises in the heart, we are safer
in the arms of the cantina lights

we fish our pockets for four more dollars
and accept two blessings in bottles

mumble to some lord somewhere to forgive us
for what we are about to do, a unison whisper

as the last boxcar stumbles into the night,
a fading sainthood, the cantina lights glowing forever.

Freight Train Through Phoenix

Jerry D. Mathes II

After school my brothers and I stood on the electric
box and stared over our safe suburban fence
at the train rumbling west past our house.
We'd count the men sitting in open rail cars, clinging
to the undercarriage, or balancing on the couplings.

The desert sun slanted at hard angles, casting dark
shadows on grimy faces and worn clothes in the folded
blacks and grays of Depression photographs. We boys
imagined riding the rails like heroic vagabonds
in the movies or books. Hobos scrounging for work

in the orchards and fields toward the coasts.
We couldn't imagine the cold bite of steel, the nonstop
vibration shaking their marrow over the miles, over
the days and nights through the relentless wind.
How could we? Kids. Know the cold burn of body heat
lost like the last few dollars spent for a loaf of bread

and a jar of peanut butter, hoping it'll feed him till the next
five dollars. The next seasonal job. We kids couldn't imagine
holding the last sandwich in the heat of a desert day.
Nibbling the crust like it was the last one on Earth.

What did we know of hunger on a freight train, rolling
through Phoenix into a sunset limited by whatever crop
was ripe? To us an empty bread bag caught in the wheels
of a west bound train was just trash, and not
the remnants of some man's last meal.

Driven to the Border

Darla McBryde

If she looks back she will see the city stretch out behind her
grow pale like a predator in chase losing breath
dank swampy greens and murky concrete grays
loosen their stranglehold as she leaves behind
cubicles and computers, accountability and appointments.
She trades the confusion of traffic reports and the blind buzz
of bottomless TV for a land of hawks and smugglers' roads.

Suburbia stalks her, jilted and stubborn,
becomes trapped in her unapologetic silage
disappears into a chorus of fading goodbyes.
Her road leads west to the heart of honest earth,
its worn shiny bones reveal tangible secrets of creation
deciphered by the inquisitive glare of suns
and the veiled surveillance of border moons.

Mountains recede and impose as cloud shadows wave their wands
The Rio Bravo is a cauldron of muddy marrow
rich enough to satiate the hunger of a wide West Texas sky.
Earth umbers and spiny cactus ochers transform
to beckoning blue vistas, her reality sharpened by
the ocotillo bloom of stark red birds, the black of ravens
and the bleached white of skulls.
She worships in the quiet of star struck night,
bathed in a holy silence thick and comforting.
She barely hears the whirling silver wheels of passing trains.

Breaker Smith

Wade Martin

I was stake-driver,
iron-pounder, heavy-on-the-line.
Stone, acres, mountains, time:
when there was an obstacle,
they'd ask for Breaker.
I was an arm and a fist,
I was a man and a myth
of the West. I was best-man
at the wedding of the oceans:
I carried a ring of steel
to the altar and laid it
in tycoon hands. At night,
bundled in burlap, bottle beside me,
I sang for the land. I was a man.
Breaker of wills and winds and hills,
master of swing and strike and rail.
But after day's last clang
echoed away down dark smooth swills,
I swayed on my bunk in hymn.

Medicine Tree

Allen Braden

A disbeliever down to the bone,
he kneels before the stunted tree
alone in the feverish desert

called sleep. Various offerings—
wells of ink, plaster statuettes,
pages yellowed by time and heat—

from those who, like him,
once hoped to be forgiven or healed
lie scattered around. No doubt

he desires the persimmon
seeds (some kind of constellation
or perhaps consolation).

Such windfallen fruit.
Such impossible mercy.
Nothing here, says coyote.

Excerpt from the Broken *Norteno Corrido*

Ken Meisel

All panic is the final end-point of holding on.
    After that, it steams right up where the panic
        is vaporized.

It's evaporated like Blanco tequila
    inside the hot guitar strings
        until the air surrounding it,

enflamed, is Tex-Mex spice:
    salsa herbs, peppers,
        onions, cooked chilli rellenos,

the pungent aroma of somebody's carnitas and salsa,
    rising and wafting
        from open-slotted kitchenettes.

The pulse and breath pumping
    of a two row button accordion.
        Silk strings of brown guitars

and mariachi fiddles, lifting up
    where beyond you,
        up in the decorated yucca gardens,

men and women
    flaunt themselves
        in mariachi dances, in celebration,

and, the wide-eyed *liaison* you saw
       (with the Calypso Orchid,
              set and pinned,

just behind the curve of her left ear
       where her hair,
             brown as caramel tequila,

fell languidly to her neck, and, her dress,
       like vein-stone vellum, clung)
             drank the Corrido heat

of the afternoon into her
       just enough to make her
             glow like a bronzed figurine,

an orchid petal – *Calypso bulbosa* –
       so that you could ache enough
             to write these songs for her.

You stood by the little plaza fountain,
       continuing on with its gentle drizzle
             of mushroom-tinted water

puddling over the edge,
       and you heard, for the first time,
             the line, *you took me by surprise*

as you watched her, under the stucco archway
       of a lonesome bodega, her gaze, like safire.
             Confetti and egg shells,

scattered all over the platform tiles,
  (after the Day of the Dead parade
    floats have run through)

and, you *did* find her – inexplicably –
  floating vaporously there,
    like an ocotillo angel in your exotic dreams,

(whether or not she was the redhead
  at the All Hallow's Guild Carnival,
    or the honeysuckle angel,

the angel de la majer,
  felled in a 64' gold metallic Rambler
    blasted into angry steam and oblivion

on the yellow line of the dusty road,)
  while the rest of you –
    caught good and quick

with your astonished face
  in the convex mirror –
    knew you could never hold her

in the rice paper light,
  or in the liquored heat:
    (– how you fell for her

magnesia-white saint's face in the parlor,
and her eyes, like radiant rose of sharon
when you lost her –)

because she's nothing more
than Norteno Corrido
invention –

(she's just the opaque face
inside the calcite crystal's
fluorescent cleft…)

Friends, all we are,
at the warping edge, in the end,
is Norteno Corrido invention.

I must tell you, we glow like fluorite flakes.
We sing the body electric,
like running silver confetti

turned-to-schools-of fish
swimming through the plaza,
just after the explosion

has occurred at the post-office.
All we are, in the end,
is Norteno Corrido invention.

We *radiate* –
       because, you see, our bodies are sealed
        with sundial kisses.

We glow like fluorite flakes.
       Our lips, dripping wet,
         something warm,

always running in our eyes.
       The car, stalled-out, dead,
         in the middle of the road –

just like you knew that it would,
       this ache of love,
         this love so strange.

If I were a carpenter, you'd be my lady…
       Let's think about tomorrow, girl,
         our future's right…

These are the songs
       I must write for you,
         my Sombrero Madonna,

my ocotillo angel
       wrapped in
         ethyl moonlight…

Friends, I must tell you, we're culled
    in dangerous rhythm.
        Nothing of us lasts.

Fingers, ignited in every fiddle solo –
    in every magic moment,
        your lips so close to mine…

All we are is h*allucination*, just sizzled after-glow
    inside the Norteno Corrido excerpt.
        Freddie Fender

hooting it up San Benito, Texas.
    (Hooting it up.)
        My moonlight Madonna,

my Sombrero Mambo of luna pearls
    and the star's radiant
        twinkling twilight,

listen to these lines I write for you,
    songs from you,
        and from within you –

But you know that I'll be there for you –
    Before the next teardrop falls…
        Will you still love me tomorrow? –

in a sea of love? – you heard me right.
    In a sea of love?
        Because we're runaways?

We wonder, why, why, why? –
> Hold me tight,
>> my Luna Madonna.

We will last forever...I will take you there.

karla k. morton, **Chimayo**

The Night We Ate the Javelina

June Blumenson

I watched you take small bites
and tip your chin
down to make it easier to swallow.
What do you think about?
I asked. Tea-lights flickered on the adobe
walls of your cactus garden, plants
carefully selected for heat
tolerance–donkey tails, golden barrels,
Mexican fence posts, and clumps of prickly
pear from which (we always say)
we will someday
make honey. I love how these common
names capture the imagination,
as if christened by a happy
heart, a full belly.
You said, I think about my limitations.

I thought about the javelina,
how its spear-like teeth
sharpen when the mouth opens and closes,
how the mothers roll
and tumble their young, their short life,
salt and pepper hair,
the spiky ruff around their necks.
I thought about what your friend told us
when he went hunting–
that you don't have to bleed
the javelina when dressing the carcass,
how he had expertly butchered
and kept the roast he gave us clean.

I thought about how you might choke
on the wild meat so roasted it in a slow
cooker and left for the afternoon
to push you in your wheelchair in the desert
botanical garden. I thought about how
the javelina leaves its scent on rocks
and tree stumps, and how we'd probably
never make honey out of prickly pear.

Dear DirecTV Hook-Up Guy—

Lisa Fay Coutley

Forgive me (it's been a year
since you were here in steel toes,
jeans, & a cowboy hat, running
tangled cable through the brick
wall of our new house in August
heat)—last night I dreamt you
accepted the water I should have
offered but instead prattled on about
a great lake three days by car behind
me, in a life I can hardly hear now.
Thirsty & tired of weaving through
a maze of clothes & DVDs, you
steered me toward that body
of freshwater—canyon reservoir
without waves or sand. Forgive me
my impatience with scorched land.
I've spent the better part of summer
tending the dregs of familiar plants,
but nothing thrives here that doesn't
push spines or thorns. I can't
cup my hands around your face
in the dream, but I keep wanting to
tell you that I tried to give enough
water, tried to churn the cracked dirt,
tried to yield one small thing to eat.
At some point, I picked up the phone
to call you—like you said I should
if I ever got lost. Instead, I coiled
the hose & hung it in the garage.

McCamey, Texas

Charles Dameron

We pulled up stakes in Sherwood
and drove the Model T west
to the dusty oil boom in Texon,
then on in '26 to the new well
further west, tents mushrooming
by the week next to the nearby
railroad siding, ten thousand of us
by the next year. Me and Annie
opened up a restaurant, which
durn near killed us, oil workers
and fancy ladies coming in all
day and night, driving us
to build and run a boarding house.
Good living till the big crash
took the town's refinery with it.
Life shrank, then limped along.
And George McCamey, who drilled
the well with Gilbert Johnson?
His name stuck when the tents
became a town, but he never lived
here, stopping by from time to time,
too busy wildcatting elsewhere
or enjoying the genteel fineries

of Fort Worth. His thumbprint's
still here, though, and the new
derricks now harvest only the wind
that blows day and night against
the letters on my gravestone.

Note: Frank Dameron opened McCamey's first restaurant in 1926. In
2001 the Texas legislature named McCamey "the Wind Energy
Capital of Texas."

Patillo Higgins, Wildcatter (1863-1955)

Clarence Wolfshohl

Old one-arm Higgins is buried there.
Plain grave, granite cross—he was zealous,
born again after that shoot-out with the deputy.
When we heard whose grave we were digging,
Roberto joked we might strike a gusher.

He was the one set off Spindletop—
knew there was oil from the smell.
They say he made millions off and on,
but Lucas or that other guy got it all
from that first gusher. It blew
for nine days—more oil than they'd take
from Pennsylvania in a year.

Higgins knew his oil, the formations
to look for, the taste of the soil.
He was always prospecting, pick
and shovel in the car trunk, from Lufkin
to McCamey and up to Borger. Searching
with that fire-eyed wildcatter gaze
for that sulphur bitterness sweet
on the tongue. Digging into the pits
of Hell to find the realm of Heaven.

'04 Playoffs

J. Scott Brownlee

Days I tossed baseballs
thinking I'd go pro someday—
play for the 'Stros, Yankees, or Mets—

I got invited to tryout, but that was it.
And yet I still remember feeling
what I can't explain to you—

5,000 fans screaming at me
from all across the Lone Star State—
something not unlike joy, although

different from it, as I stepped
on the mound. The whole town
came and clapped for us despite

the fact, ultimately, we lost:
beaten miserably. The fans
I still want to remember

cheered us on, whereas
the true town that existed
up and left about the second

or the third. Only my parents
and a few sports writers stayed
to watch the Leopards of La Grange

defeat the Llano Yellow Jackets
with our silly orange socks
by ten-run rule: eleven zip.

When that embarrassment
was over, everyone received
bronze medals, and I knelt down

on the baseline with the blue bag
Larry Don, my coach, gave me.
I scooped up dirt, gathering it

because I wanted to remember
our epic failure: white hatbands
caked in thick layers of sweat—

the plush hotel they put us in
before the game, the way it rained.
My teammate trying on his bathrobe

at the Omni: poor enough to know
he'd never have a plush bathrobe
like that for the rest of his life.

And walking out on Disch-Faulk Field
where college baseball games were played,
and knowing none of us would ever play

again. None of us made it to the pros,
and yet at that point we believed
that we would each go all the way

because the town said, *You are gods.*
We believe in you kids. You are unstoppable.
Our first time being on TV none of us

knew how smack was talked and so claimed
Homer Bailey couldn't pitch for shit
despite the fact the papers said he'd go

in the first round. *Where are you from?*
reporters asked. *And can you win, possibly,*
do you think? Of course, we said spitting dip,

swaggering. It was the first time
and the last with our butch bravado
and our broad teenage grins—

our girlfriends going down on us
the same way we went down on them
in truck beds shaking with the weight

of bodies arcing six inches away
from each other—we told the truth
innocently. Those nights we loosened

slick, scarlet-red seams, making naked
the ball, compressed cork and cowhide
at the heart of the game we realized

joy might be given base runners, signs
uncrossed, green lights to swing—no hit-
and-run or safety squeeze—if we only let it.

American Palimpsest

Greg Emilio

For a week I drove away from sunsets,
losing hours in the rearview's afterburn,

the diffuse oil slicks of evenfall fading
behind the U-haul as I headed east.

I confess I left California without conflict,
wildfire, the grist of a fugitive narrative.

But I found meaning in the ubiquitous
black-eyed Susans along the median,

the flashing runnel of yellow flowers
ceaseless across the great Southwest.

I felt as American as the silos of Texas,
those towering patinas of rust and open sky,

awestruck by the thunderstorms and greenery,
pure, confounding, of dustbowl Oklahoma.

In Arkansas coyotes punctuated the highway
with fly-spangled carcasses. In Mississippi

dead armadillos seemed to sink into the road,
yowling in hallowed, last-ditch rictuses.

In Alabama, a feathery Monarch managed
to wrap its spindled body around the antenna:

ephemera folded, atrophied in wind
that carried me then, and only then.

The Blues stations of Tennessee vacillated
in & out to a metronome of white lines.

But the road needs more than love songs;
America manifested deserves forgiveness.

We need new ways to bless the caesuras
of land between gas stations, state lines.

We need stories firm as blacktop underfoot:
a couple on the lam, blood more red than wine.

We need modern epics for our busking,
not this suitcase of half-erased sketches.

Blue Horse Press Archives, **The Crossing at Garlock**

In Memoriam

Andrea Alfier

May 23, 1929 – February 4, 2016

Madeline Defrees

November 18, 1919 – November 11, 2015

SPRING 2016 CONTRIBUTORS

Pamela Ahlen is program coordinator for Bookstock (Woodstock, Vermont), the Green Mountain Literary Festival. She organizes literary events for Osher (Lifelong Education at Dartmouth). Pam received an MFA in creative writing from Vermont College of Fine Arts. She is the author of the chapbook *Gather Every Little Thing* (Finishing Line Press). She lives with her husband near the Appalachian Trail in Barnard, VT.

Doug Anderson's first book of poems, *The Moon Reflected Fire,* won the Kate Tufts Discovery Award and his second, *Blues for Unemployed Secret Police* a grant from the Academy of American Poets. His memoir, *Keep Your Head Down: Vietnam, the Sixties and a Journey of Self-Discovery,* was published by W. W. Norton in 2009. His most recent book of poems is *Horse Medicine.* He has taught in the MFA programs at the Pacific University of Oregon and Bennington College, Smith College, and the University of Massachusetts.

Shaun Asbury is a two-time graduate of Youngstown State University. His work has appeared in *Kestrel.* A Kansas native, he currently calls Tucson, AZ home.

Carol Barrett has earned doctorates in both creative writing and clinical psychology. Her books include <u>Calling in the Bones</u>, which won the Snyder Prize from Ashland Poetry Press. An NEA grant recipient in poetry, she teaches in the Humanities and Culture major for Union Institute & University. The poems submitted to this issue of the journal were all written during a residency at Ghost Ranch, New Mexico.

David J. Bauman's poems have appeared in various journals including *Contemporary American Voices*, *The Blue Hour Magazine, T(OUR)*, and *Word Fountain*. He has recent work published or forthcoming from Kind of a Hurricane Press and *Watershed, a Journal of the Susquehanna*. His awards include the Savage Poetry Prize from Bloomsburg University and the Academy of American Poets.

Kyce Bello edited the anthology *The Return of the River: Writers, Scholars, and Citizens Speak on Behalf of the Santa Fe River* (Sunstone Press, 2011), which won two New Mexico Book Awards. She is an MFA candidate at the Institute of American Indian Arts, and lives with her family in Santa Fe, NM.

Alan Birkelbach is the winner of the 2015 Spur Award for Best Western Poem from the Western Writers of America. He is a member of both the Texas Institute of Letters and The Academy of American Poets. He has ten collections of poetry. He is the 2005 Poet Laureate of Texas.

June Blumenson's work appears in *Adana Literary Journal, Boston Literary Magazine, Comstock, The French Literary Review, Intimate Landscapes, Literal Latte* contest, *The Edge*, The Loft/Minneapolis Institute of Art contest, *Nimrod International Journal* contest, *Times They Were A-Changing*, and *Snowy Egret*. She is a member of Minnesota Poetry Therapy Network, Loft Literary Center, teaches poetry classes and curates a poetry reading series at a community center in Minneapolis.

Allen Braden is the author of *A Wreath of Down and Drops of Blood* and *Elegy in the Passive Voice*. He has received fellowships from the NEA and Artist Trust. Assistant poetry editor of *Terrain.org: A Journal of the Built + Natural Environments*, he teaches at Tacoma Community College and volunteers for AWP's Writer to Writer mentorship program.

Jerry Bradley, winner of the 2015 Boswell Poetry Prize, is poetry editor of *Concho River Review* and the author of 3 poetry collections. His poetry has appeared in *New England Review, Modern Poetry Studies, Poetry Magazine*, and *Southern Humanities Review*.

Bernard Briggs is originally from Sussex, a county in the south of England, but now lives in the city of Aberdeen in the north east of Scotland, with his wife Mandy. He has been writing poetry since he was a schoolboy and has had three collections published in the UK.

J. Scott Brownlee is a former Writers in the Public Schools Fellow at New York University, where he taught poetry to undergraduates and fifth graders through the Teachers & Writers Collaborative. He is the author of three prize-winning chapbooks: *Highway or Belie*ı (Button Poetry, 2014), *Ascension* (Texas Review Press, 2015); and *On the Occasion of the Last Old Camp Meeting in Llano County* (Tree Light Books, 2015). *Requiem for Used Ignition Cap* (Orison Books, 2015), his first full-length collection, was a finalist for the National Poetry Series and selected by C. Dale Young as the winner of the inaugural Orison Poetry Prize. He is a founding member of The Localists and lives in Philadelphia.

JV Brummels' fifth full-length collection, *City at War,* was published by The Backwaters Press in late 2009. His work has been recognized with a Literature Fellowship from the National Endowment for the Arts, the Elkhorn Prize and the Mildred Bennett Award for contributions to the state's literature from the Nebraska Center for the Book. His *Book of Grass* was awarded the 2008 Nebraska Book Award for Poetry. Raised first on a farm and later on a ranch, he was educated at the University of Nebraska and later Syracuse University. In 1984 he and his family began a horseback cattle outfit to raise natural, grass-fed beef, which they continue to operate as Lightning Creek Cattle Company. A longtime professor at Wayne State College, home of the longest running poetry slam west of Chicago, he's also written and published short fiction and a novel. For the last 20 years he's served as publisher of Logan House, co-founded with Jim Reese, which specializes in contemporary American poetry. In 2006 he was named co-director of the newly created WSC Press.

David Chorlton is a 36-year resident of Arizona, having moved from the old world. He currently has poems as part of the "Fires of Change" exhibition at Tucson's U of A Art Museum, shown through March of this year. His book "A Field Guide to Fire" is his contribution to the project.

Kevin Marshall Chopson received his M.F.A. from Murray State University and is a three-time Pushcart Prize nominee. His work has appeared in *Poetry Salzburg Review* (Austria), *Nashville Arts Magazine, Nazar Look* (Romania), *The Broad River Review, English Journal, The Southern Poetry Anthology, Number One, English Journal, Saint Katherine Review, I-70 Review,* and in previous issues of

San Pedro River Review, among numerous others. Chopson teaches writing at Davidson Academy and Volunteer State Community College, both just north of Nashville, Tennessee.

Paul Christensen has just published his eight book of poems, THE JACK OF POEMS IS A HARD CARD TO PLAY (Lamar University Press), all about the light and dark of the complicated state of Texas. His previous collection, THE HUMAN CONDITION (Wings Press) was a finalist in the Texas Institute of Letters annual poetry award. He has written scores of essays for *Antioch Review*, *Southwest Review*, and other journals, as well as short stories and commentaries. His blog at paul-christensen.com covers many subjects from politics to pobiz and mass culture.

Will Cordeiro's work appears or is forthcoming in *BOAAT*, *Copper Nickel*, *Cortland Review*, *Crab Orchard Review*, *CutBank Online*, *DIAGRAM*, *Drunken Boat*, *Fourteen Hills*, *Harpur Palate*, *New Madrid*, *Phoebe*, *Valparaiso Poetry Review*, and elsewhere. He lives in Flagstaff, Arizona, where he is a faculty member in the Honors Program at Northern Arizona University.

Lisa Fay Coutley is the author of *Errata* (Southern Illinois University Press, 2015), winner of the Crab Orchard Series in Poetry Open Competition, and *In the Carnival of Breathing* (Black Lawrence Press, 2011), winner of the Black River Chapbook Competition. Her poems have been awarded a fellowship from the National Endowment for the Arts, scholarships to the Sewanee and Bread Loaf Writers' Conferences, and an Academy of American Poets Levis Prize. Recent poetry and prose publications include *Prairie Schooner, Crab Orchard Review, Kenyon Review, Crazyhorse, Gulf Coast,* & *Poets & Writers.* At present, she is the Visiting Assistant Professor in Poetry at the University of Oregon.

Jerry Craven has published 26 books including poetry, fiction, and nonfiction. He lives in Jasper, Texas with his wife, the poet Sherry Craven. Currently he serves as director of Lamar University Press and Ink Brush Press and is editor-in-chief of the online journal *Amarillo Bay.* www.jerrycraven.com

Chip Dameron is the author of a travel book and seven collections of poetry, including two published in 2015: *Waiting for an Etcher* (Lamar University Press) and *Drinking from the River: New and Selected Poems, 1975-2015* (Wings Press). His poems, as well as his essays on contemporary writers, have appeared in numerous journals and anthologies in the U.S. and abroad. He is a two-time nominee for the Pushcart Prize and a member of the Texas Institute of Letters. A professor emeritus of English at The University of Texas Rio Grande Valley, he lives and writes in Brownsville, Texas.

Taylor Leigh D'Amico is a Georgia native who writes poetry, fiction, and nonfiction. She is also a student of theater and film. She earned her BA in English from Kennesaw State University and currently studies writing with William Wright. "Reformation" is her debut publication.

William Virgil Davis's most recent book of poetry is *Dismantlements of Silence: Poems Selected and New* (2015). He has published five other books of poetry: *The Bones Poems*, *Landscape and Journey*, which won the New Criterion Poetry Prize and the Helen C. Smith Memorial Award for Poetry; *Winter Light*; *The Dark Hours*, which won the Calliope Press Chapbook Prize; *One Way to Reconstruct the Scene*, which won the Yale Series of Younger Poets Prize. His poems have appeared in most of the major periodicals, here and abroad, including *Agenda, The Atlantic Monthly, The Gettysburg Review, The Georgia Review, The Harvard Review, The Hopkins Review, The Hudson Review The Nation, The New Criterion, PN Review, Poetry, The Sewanee Review, Southwest Review, The Southern Review*, and *TriQuarterly,* among many others.

Steve Dieffenbacher's full-length book of poems, *The Sky Is a Bird of Sorrow,* was published by Wordcraft of Oregon in 2012. The collection won a ForeWord Reviews 2013 Bronze Award for poetry. A poem in the book, "Night Singer, Chaco Canyon, New Mexico," was named a 2013 Spur Award poetry finalist by the Western Writers of America. He also has won journalism honors in feature writing and photography. He lives in Medford, Oregon.

Matthew Dulany has previously contributed to *SPRR*. Other poems of his have appeared in *South Carolina Review* and *The Sow's Ear,* short stories in *Ontario Review* and *RipRap*. His first novel, *The Quitter*, is forthcoming from Hard Nock Press.

James H Duncan is the editor of *Hobo Camp Review* and the author of such books as *What Lies In Wait*, *Berlin*, and *Dealing With the Devil in the Middle of the Road*. For more of his work, visit www.jameshduncan.com

S.J. Dunning lives in Tacoma, Washington. She is Co-Editor-in-Chief and Nonfiction Editor of *5x5 Literary Magazine* and teaches English online. Previous work of hers has appeared in *The Boiler*, *Front Porch Journal*, *Dogwood*, *Creative Nonfiction*, and other journals.

Greg Emilio is a Southern California native whose poetry and essays have appeared or are forthcoming in *Miramar*, *Permafrost*, *Pleiades*, and *World Literature Today*. In 2015 he won the Pangaea Prize from The Poets Billow. A devout bon vivant, he currently bartends while pursuing his PhD in English at Georgia State University in Atlanta.

Susan J. Erickson recently completed a manuscript of poems in women's voices. Her poems appear in *2River View*, *Crab Creek Review*, *The Fourth River*, *Naugatuck River Review*, *Raven Chronicles* and *The James Franco Review*. Susan lives in Bellingham, Washington where she helped to establish the Sue C. Boynton Poetry Walk.

Alexis Rhone Fancher's poem, "when I turned fourteen, my mother's sister took me to lunch and said:" was chosen by Edward Hirsch for inclusion in *The Best American Poetry of 2016*.
She is the author of *How I Lost My Virginity To Michael Cohen and other heart stab poems,* (Sybaritic Press, 2014), and *State of Grace: The Joshua Elegics,* (KYSO Flash Press, 2015). Find her poems in *Rattle, The MacGuffin, Slipstream, Wide Awake: Poets of Los Angeles, Chiron Review, HOBART,* and elsewhere. Her photographs have been published worldwide. Since 2013 she's been nominated for six Pushcart Prizes and four Best of The Net awards. Alexis is poetry editor of *Cultural Weekly,* where she also publishes a monthly photo essay, *The Poet's Eye*. Find her at alexisrhonefancher.com

Lisha Adela García is a poet who has México, the United States and the land in between in her work. She has an MFA from Vermont College in Writing and currently resides in Texas with her beloved four legged children. Lisha has a chapbook entitled, *This Stone Will Speak*, from Pudding House Press and a book, *Blood Rivers*, from Blue Light Press of San Francisco and other multiple publications.

Rohan Garg is currently a junior in high school who lives near Cleveland, Ohio. In addition to pursuing his passion for photography, he is a co-editor of his school's yearly literary journal. As a photographer, he is most interested in nature macrophotography, rural landscape photography, and photography of urban spaces. His works have previously been published in *Pea River Journal, The Decades Review, Portland Review, The Sonder Review,* and *Oxford Magazine,* among other magazines. Additionally, he has won the Scholastic Gold Key Award in Photography, the Cleveland Institute of Art Special Recognition Award, and an Honorable Mention in the 2D3D National Art Competition.

Reuven Goldfarb is a writer, teacher, and rabbinic deputy, Reuven has published *Divrei Torah,* poetry, essays, and stories in numerous periodicals and anthologies and won several awards. He co-founded and edited *AGADA,* the illustrated Jewish literary magazine (1981-88), and taught Freshman English in Oakland's Merritt College (1989-1996). He and his wife have resided in the Upper Galilee since 2001.

Kevin Goodan was raised in western Montana, and fought forest fires for ten seasons with the USFS, on the Lolo National Forest. He is the author of *In The Ghost-House Acquainted, Winter Tenor, Upper Level Disturbances,* and the forthcoming *Let The Voices.* He is Associate Professor of English at Lewis-Clark State College.

Jack Granath is a librarian in Kansas.

John Grey is an Australian poet, US resident. Recently published in *New Plains Review, Perceptions* and the anthology, *No Achilles* with work upcoming in Big Muddy Review, *Gargoyle, Coal City Review* and *Nebo.*

Ken Hada has six books of poetry in print, including *Persimmon Sunday* (VAC, 2015). His *Spare Parts* received the 2011 Wrangler Award from the National Western Heritage Museum. His poem "Homecoming" was a 2015 finalist for the Spur award. Reviews and information may be found at: www.kenhada.org

Marian Haddad is a Pushcart-nominated poet who published a chapbook, *Saturn Falling Down (2003),* at the request of Texas Public Radio, in correlation with their Hands-on Poetry workshops, which she taught. Her first full-length poetry collection, *Somewhere between Mexico and a River Called Home* (Pecan Grove Press, 2004) approached its 5th printing before the passing of editor, H. Palmer Hall, a Small Press Review Notable Book. PGP also published her poetry collection, *Wildflower. Stone.* (2011), their first hardback in the press' twenty-five years, and is endorsed by Yusef Komonyakaa. A visiting writer and lecturer, she's completed her fourth poetry manuscript, which will print at 160 pages, *In this City of Saints* (Mouthfeel Press, Autumn 2016); she's completing a collection of poetry, *Tourmaline: Considerations on the Shroud of Turin* and is working on a poetry collection about her father's diagnosis and passing, *Gravity.* A collection of personal essays is in-progress, *These Languages inside Our House.* Her work has appeared in a number of anthologies/journals, most recently in two Mutabilis Press anthologies, Knot [online journal], BorderSenses, and is forthcoming in Crab Orchard Review.

Carol Hamilton has published 17 books: children's novels, legends and poetry, most recently, Such Deaths. She is a former Poet Laureate of Oklahoma and has been nominated six times for a Pushcart Prize. Upcoming works are in *Poet Lore*, *Louisiana Literature*, *Limestone*, and others.

Chera Hammons is a graduate of the MFA in Creative Writing program at Goddard College in Plainfield, VT. Her work has recently appeared in *Beloit Poetry Journal, Heron Tree, Rattle, San Pedro River Review, Tupelo Quarterly,* and *Valparaiso Poetry Review,* among other fine journals. Her chapbook *Amaranthine Hour* received the 2012 Jacar Press Chapbook Award, and her full-length book *Recycled Explosions* is forthcoming from Ink Brush Press. She is a member of the editorial board of poetry journal *One*. She lives in Amarillo, TX and teaches at Clarendon College.

Luke J. Johnson lives with his feisty Italian wife and two babies, in San Luis Obispo, California. He has a crush on John Coltrane, loves Monk, Charlie "Bird Parker, abandoned box cars, Jack Kerouac's voice, and believes bonds formed around bourbon, are thicker than blood.

John Lambremont, Sr. is a poet and writer from Baton Rouge, Louisiana, U.S.A., where he serves as editor of Big River Poetry Review, see bigriverpoetry.com. John has a B.A. in Creative Writing and a J.D. from Louisiana State University. His work has been published internationally in many reviews and anthologies, including *The Minetta Review, Clarion, The Chaffin Journal, The Mayo Review, Picayune, The Louisiana Review,* and *Words & Images,* and he has been nominated for The Pushcart Prize. John's second full-length poetry collection is <u>Dispelling The Indigo Dream</u> (Local Gems Poetry Press, 2013), and his latest poetry chapbook, <u>What It Means To Be A Man (And Other Poems Of Life And Death)</u>, was published in December 2014 by Finishing Line Press.

Alex Lemon's most recent book is *The Wish Book*. He is the author of *Happy: A Memoir* (Scribner) and three other poetry collections: *Mosquito, Hallelujah Blackout,* and *Fancy Beasts*. An essay collection and a fifth poetry book are forthcoming from Milkweed Editions. His writing has appeared in *Esquire, American Poetry Review, The Huffington Post, Ploughshares, Best American Poetry, Tin House, Kenyon Review, AGNI, New England Review, The Southern Review* and *jubilat,* among others. Among his awards are a 2005 Fellowship in Poetry from the NEA and a 2006 Minnesota Arts Board Grant. He is an editor-at-large for Saturnalia Books, the poetry editor of *descant,* sits on the the editorial board of TCU press and *The Southern Review*. He lives in Ft. Worth, Texas, writes book reviews for the *Dallas Morning News,* and teaches at TCU and in Ashland University's Low-Residency MFA program.

Widely anthologized and the author of a dozen books, **Adrian C. Louis's** poems have been published in many of the leading literary magazines in America including *The Kenyon Review, Ploughshares,*

New Letters, The Antioch Review, The Nebraska Review, North Dakota Quarterly, The Nation, Chicago Review, Chelsea, TriQuarterly, Crazyhorse, The Southern Review, The Missouri Review, Midwest Quarterly, Prairie Schooner, Poetry Daily, and *The North American Review.*

Peter Ludwin, a 2016 Finalist for the Tucson Festival of Books Literary Awards in the poetry category, is the recipient of a Literary Fellowship from Artist Trust and the W.D. Snodgrass Poetry Award for Endeavor and Excellence. The latter was conferred by the directors of the San Miguel Poetry Week in San Miguel de Allende, Mexico, which he attended for twelve years, workshopping under such noted poets as Mark Doty, Tony Hoagland, Joseph Stroud and Robert Wrigley. His two books are *A Guest in All Your Houses,* which is set in the Southwest, and *Rumors of Fallible Gods,* a two-time Finalist for the Gival Press Poetry Award. His work can be found in *Atlanta Review, Concho River Review, Naugatuck River Review, Santa Fe Literary Review* and *Soundings Review,* among many other journals. His next book, *Gone to Gold Mountain,* is forthcoming this year from MoonPath Press.

Kaitlin LaMoine Martin was raised by a community of writers in Kalamazoo, Michigan. She's been published in *Passages North, Bellevue Literary Review,* and *Borderlands: Texas Poetry Review,* among others. She owns a photography business, works for Communities In Schools, and spends hours thinking of new ways to entertain her dogs, Frida and Adam Lee Wags II.

Wade Martin is co-editor of the *Texas Poetry Calendar* and a 2014 Pushcart nominee. He is also a Teaching Artist with Badgerdog and archivist at Austin Community College, with recent publications in *Perfume River Poetry Review, Freshwater,* and *Bird's Thumb.*

Jerry D. Mathes II a Jack Kent Cooke alumnus and is the author *Ahead of the Flaming Front: A Life on Fire*, winner of the North American Book Prize; an essay collection *Fever and Guts: A Symphony*; *The Journal West: Poems*, and *Still Life*, the winner of the Meadow Prize for the Novella. His photography, poems, essays, and short stories, have won numerous awards. In 2011, he produced a short film, "Drinking

197

Sangria in the Cold War," which was adapted from one of his award winning short stories. He has worked as a martial arts instructor, an armor crewman, a construction worker, hotel auditor, car salesman, repo-man, delivery guy, cable guy, went logging, worked in forestry, crewed on several types of fishing vessels, fought wildfire on a helicopter-rappel crew, taught writing at the University of Idaho and Stephen F. Austin State University and taught the Southernmost Writers Workshop in the World at Amundsen-Scott South Pole Station Antarctica during the 2009-2010 and 2011-2012 Austral summer seasons where he worked in logistics. He also wrote and directed two short films while at the South Pole. In 2012 he produced a video essay about wildfire. He loves his two daughters very much.

Darla McBryde lives in Alpine, Texas. She was chosen as a feature for the Houston Library's Public Poetry program and the Houston performance poetry group "Word Around Town". She is a recipient of the Houston Poetry Fest's Lorene Pouncey Award and is a Pushcart Nominee. Her work has appeared in the Texas Poetry Calendar, San Pedro River Review, Illya's Honey, Cenizo Journal and others. She has published 4 chapbooks.

Bukowski's Indian pal Dave Reeve, editor of *Zen Tattoo* gave **Catfish McDaris** his name when he spoke of wanting to quit the post office and start a catfish farm. He spent a summer shark fishing in the Sea of Cortez, built adobe houses, tamed wild horses around the Grand Canyon, worked in a zinc smelter in the panhandle of Texas, and painted flag poles in the wind.

David Meischen has had poems in *The Southern Review, Southern Poetry Review, San Pedro River Review,* and elsewhere. A Pushcart nominee, he is co-founder of Dos Gatos Press, publisher of *Wingbeats* and *Wingbeats II,* collections of poetry writing exercises. His short stories have appeared in *The Gettysburg Review* and *Bellingham Review,* among others.

Ken Meisel is a poet from the Detroit area, a 2012 Kresge Arts Literary Fellow, and a Pushcart Prize nominee with publications in *Rattle, San Pedro River Review, Boxcar Review, Midwest Gothic* and *Pirene's Fountain.* His books include *The Drunken Sweetheart at My Door*

(FutureCycle Press: 2015), *Scrap Metal Mantra Poems* (Main Street Rag: 2013), and *Beautiful Rust* (Bottom Dog Press: 2009).

Megan Merchant is the author of *Translucent, sealed.* (Dancing Girl Press, 2015), *In the Rooms of a Tiny House* (ELJ Publications, October 2016), *Gravel Ghosts* (Glass Lyre Press, Spring 2016) and the 2015 Lyrebird Prize winning book *The Dark's Humming* (Glass Lyre Press, 2017). She has a children's book forthcoming through Philomel Books and teaches at Prescott College.

Jeanetta Calhoun Mish's most most recent books are *Oklahomeland: Essays* (Lamar University Press, 2015) and a poetry collection, *What I Learned at the War* (West End Press, March 2016). Jeanetta is editor Mongrel Empire Press and contributing editor to *Sugar Mule* (www.sugarmule.com) and *Oklahoma Today.* She is director of The Red Earth Creative Writing MFA Program at Oklahoma City University.

karla k. morton, the 2010 Texas Poet Laureate, is a Councilor of the Texas Institute of Letters, member of the Western Writers of America, and graduate of Texas A&M University. Described as "one of the most adventurous voices in American poetry," she is a Betsy Colquitt Award Winner, twice an Indie National Book Award Winner, a North Texas Book Award Festival Winner, and Finalist for the Montaigne Medal. Morton is the recipient of the Writer-in-Residency E2C Grant and has ten collections of poetry. She is widely published, is a nominee for the National Cowgirl Hall of Fame, and established an ekphrastic collaborative touring exhibit titled *No End of Vision,* pairing photography with poetry. Morton's work has been used by many students in their UIL Contemporary Poetry contests, and was featured with seven other prominent authors in *8 Voices: Contemporary Poetry of the American Southwest* (from Baskerville Publications), which is now part of the SMU teaching curriculum. Recently, Morton has become one of the first twelve inductees to Denton, Texas *Arts Walk of Fame*, along with Norah Jones, O'Neil Ford, Ray Wylie Hubbard, Pat Boone and others. Her forthcoming book by Texas Review Press, *Accidental Origami: New and Selected Work* by karla k. morton is due to be released Spring 2016.

Benjamin Myers is the 2015-2016 Poet Laureate of Oklahoma and the author of two volumes of poetry: *Lapse Americana* (New York Quarterly Books, 2013) and *Elegy for Trains* (Village Books Press, 2010). His poems may be read in *The Yale Review, 32 Poems, Image* and other journals. Myers teaches creative writing and literature at Oklahoma Baptist University, where he is the Crouch-Mathis Professor of Literature.

Steve Myers has published a full-length collection, *Memory's Dog*, and two chapbooks. A Pushcart Prize winner, his poems have previously appeared in journals such as *Beloit Poetry Journal, The Gettysburg Review, Poetry East, The Southern Review,* and *Tar River Poetry*. His manuscript entitled *Last Look at Joburg* recently won *The Tusculum Review*'s 2015 Poetry Chapbook Prize.

Jim Natal is the Pushcart Prize-nominated author of *52 Views: The Haibun Variations, Memory and Rain,* and two previous poetry collections. His work has appeared in many journals and anthologies, including *Hayden's Ferry Review, Spillway,* and *New Poets of the American West*. He teaches the annual Plein Air Poetry Workshop at Joshua Tree NP and directs The Literary Southwest series at Yavapai College in Prescott, AZ.

Naomi Shihab Nye was elected a Chancellor of the Academy of American Poets in 2009. Her latest book is *Famous*, a poetry and art collaboration with book illustrator Lisa Desimini.

David Olsen's *Unfolding Origami* (80pp, 2015) won the Cinnamon Press Poetry Collection Award. His three poetry chapbooks are from US publishers, and his poems appear in leading journals and anthologies on both sides of the Atlantic.

Fabrice Poussin is a Professor of French and English at a small liberal arts university, in Northern Georgia. His passion for photography and travel developed when he was 14, and ever since, he has been working to capture what people usually don't have time to contemplate. His wish is to immortalize the passing details as they may very well be what the "big picture" relies upon.

Vanessa Zimmer-Powell, a Houston poet, was the winner of a Rick Steve's Haiku Award, and was a poetry award winner at the 2013 Austin International Poetry Fest. Vanessa's poetry has been published in local and national anthologies and journals. In 2015 her work was accepted for publication in the *Avocet Weekly*, the *Avocet Journal*, *Borderlands: Texas Poetry Review*, *Copperfield Review*, *Ekphrasis*, the *Texas Poetry Calendar*, *Untameable City: Poems on the Nature of Houston*, and an upcoming anthology of persona poems of the Southwest by Dos Gatos Press.

Erin Elkins Radcliffe's poems have appeared or are forthcoming in *Hayden's Ferry Review*, *Smartish Pace*, *Nashville Review*, *Tupelo Quarterly*, and *Coal Hill Review*. Originally from Indiana, Erin now lives in Albuquerque, New Mexico, and is the author of "Station of Rain" (*Dancing Girl Press*, 2013).

Dale Ritterbusch is the author of *Lessons Learned: The Aftermath Poetry of the Vietnam War and Its Aftermath* and *Far From the Temple of Heaven*. He is a Professor of English at the University of Wisconsin-Whitewater and twice served as Distinguished Visiting Professor at the United States Air Force Academy.

Susan Rooke has recent poems in *Texas Poetry Calendar 2015* and the anthologies *Pushing the Envelope: Epistolary Poems* (ed. Jonas Zdanys, Lamar University Press 2015) and *Grit, Gravity and Grace: New Poems about Medicine and Healthcare* (ed. Rhonda L. Soricelli, M.D. and Jack Coulehan, M.D., M.P.H.; College of Physicians of Philadelphia 2015). Thrice nominated for a Pushcart and once for Best of the Net, she lives in the country near Thorndale, Texas.

Kathy Rudin is an artist from New York City. Her work has been published in, *OUT*, *Genre*, *Wilde*, *Riding Light*, *DUM-DUM*, *Rip/Torn*, *RIPRAP Journal*, *The Sun*, *The Boiler Journal* and *Bop Dead City*, among others, and has been exhibited at galleries in New York City, Miami, Los Angeles, and Vancouver.

Sheila Sanderson is a rural Kentucky native who now lives in the high desert mountains of Arizona and teaches at Prescott College. She also serves as poetry and creative nonfiction editor for *Alligator Juniper*.

Her work has appeared journals such as *Alaska Quarterly Review, Crazyhorse, Hubbub, Miramar,* and *Spillway* as well as in anthologies such as *Language Lessons* (Third Man Press), *One for the Money: The Sentence as a Poetic Form* (Lynx House Press), and *Poets of the West and West Coast* (*Southern Poetry Review*). She is the author of a collection of poetry, *Keeping Even* (Stephen F. Austin University Press).

Steven Schroeder is a poet and visual artist who has spent many years moonlighting as a philosophy professor. He grew up in the Texas Panhandle and currently lives in Chicago. His newest collection is *the moon, not the finger, pointing* (Lamar University Literary Press). More at stevenschroeder.org.

Jan Selving's poems have been published in various journals including *Ploughshares, Crazyhorse,* and *Antioch Review.* She is a visual artist as well, working in a variety of media. She currently resides in Stroudsburg, PA and teaches creative writing, women's literature, and contemporary literature at East Stroudsburg University of Pennsylvania.

Eric Paul Shaffer is author of Lāhaina Noon and Portable Planet. His poems appear in Slate, North American Review, Ploughshares, Poetry East, Rattle, The Sun Magazine, and reviews in Australia, Canada, England, Ireland, Japan, New Zealand, Scotland, and Wales. He teaches composition, literature, and creative writing at Honolulu Community College.

Ciara Shuttleworth was born in San Francisco and grew up in Nebraska, Nevada, and Washington state. Her poetry has been published in journals and anthologies, including *Alaska Quarterly Review, Confrontation, The New Yorker, The Norton Introduction to Literature 11e, Ploughshares,* and *The Southern Review.* Shuttleworth received an MFA in poetry from University of Idaho, a BFA in painting/drawing from San Francisco Art Institute, and a BA in studio art from Gustavus Adolphus College. She was a 2014 Jerome Foundation Fellow at the Anderson Center at Tower View, and The Jack Kerouac Project of Orlando's 51st resident at Jack Kerouac House.

Red Shuttleworth's most recent poetry collection, *Woe to the Land Shadowing*, came out in late 2015 from Blue Horse Press. He is a three-time winner of the Spur Award (from Western Writers of America) for Poetry. Shuttleworth was named "Best Living Western Poet" by *True West* magazine in 2007.

Marilyn Stablein is a writer and artist who works primarily in collage, assemblage and artist books. Her art appears on the covers of *Rattle* magazine, *Gargoyle*, *Malpais Review*, *Raven Chronicles* and in books and journals. Her last book of poems: *Splitting Hard Ground* won the New Mexico Poetry Award. She lives in Portland, Oregon.

Tim Staley completed a Poetry MFA from New Mexico State University in 2004. His chapbooks are available for purchase at the Grandma Moses Press online store. His hobbies include thinking, eating taquitos, and waiting. Actually, just taquitos.

Charles A. Stone was born in Green Bay, Wisconsin. He earned doctoral degrees from Marquette University and Johns Hopkins University. During his academic career he authored numerous scientific articles and edited several medical textbooks. His poetry has appeared in regional journals and anthologies. He is currently on the Board of Directors for the Austin International Poetry Festival.

Bradley R. Strahan, Taught poetry at Georgetown Univ. for 12 years; 2002-4 was Fulbright Professor of Poetry & American Culture in the Balkans. For 37 years editor/publisher of Visions-International and has 6 books of poetry & over 600 poems published worldwide. His recent book, This Art of Losing, received critical praise, and has been translated into French. His latest poetry book, about his year in Ireland, "A Parting Glass" was also translated into French.

Nano Taggart works in development for the Utah Shakespeare Festival and as a founding editor of *Sugar House Review*. He's had some stuff published elsewhere under his given name, Nathaniel, but he's tired of the Ayn Rand jokes.

Charles Thielman was born and raised in Charleston, S.C., moved to Chicago, educated at red-bricked universities and on city streets, married on a Kauai beach in 2011, a loving grandfather for six free spirits, his work as poet and shareholder in an independent Bookstore's collective continues! Google his name to read more of his poetry!

David E. Thomas grew up on the Hi-Line in North-central Montana. He graduated from the University of Montana then found himself on the streets of San Francisco where he began his literary education. Economic realities drove him to work on railroad gangs, big construction projects like Libby Dam and other labor intensive jobs. He has traveled in the United States, Mexico and Central America. He has published four books of poems, *Fossil Fuel, Buck's Last Wreck, The Hellgate Wind* and *Waterworks Hill.* He has poems in the anthologies *The Last Best Place* and *Poems across the Big Sky* and *New Poets of the American West* and has recently published poems in Romania, *Blue Collar Review* and *Cedilla 6, 7* and *8.* Most recently his essay "Gothic Days" appeared in *The Complete Montana Gothic* edited by Peter Koch which also features Thomas's earliest published work. He currently lives in Missoula, Montana.

Larry D. Thomas, who grew up in Midland, Texas, on the northeastern fringe of the Great Chihuahuan Desert, moved back to the desert in 2011 after residing for forty-four years in Houston, Texas. His poems in this issue titled "Great Horned Owl" and "Balmorhea Lake" will also appear in his chapbook, *The Innkeeper*, to be released by Mouthfeel Press in 2016. "The Visitation" is included in his chapbook, *Los Días de los Muertos* (*Right Hand Pointing* 2015). Among his other poetry collections inspired by his reverence for the Great Southwest are *Amazing Grace* (*Texas Review* Press 2001); *Where Skulls Speak Wind* (*Texas Review* Press 2004); *Stark Beauty* (Timberline Press 2005); *The Red, Candlelit Darkness* (El Grito del Lobo Press 2011, republished online in 2013 by *Right Hand Pointing*); *Far: West Texas* (*Right Hand Pointing* 2011); *The Goatherd* (Mouthfeel Press 2014); and *Art Museums* (Blue Horse Press 2014). Thomas, a member of the Texas Institute of Letters, was privileged to serve as the 2008 Texas Poet Laureate. His *As If Light Actually Matters: New & Selected Poems* was published in 2015 by *Texas Review* Press (Member, Texas A&M University Press Consortium). He resides in Alpine, Texas, with his wife, Lisa, and two Long-haired Chihuahuas, Piñon and Pecos.

Lisa P. Thomas, DDS, has enjoyed photography for several years. Her credits include *Amazing Grace* (*Texas Review* Press, 2001), *Where Skulls Speak Wind* (*Texas Review* Press, 2004), *Stark Beauty* (Timberline Press, 2005), *The Fraternity of Oblivion* (Timberline Press, 2008), *Far (West Texas)* (e-chapbook/*Right Hand Pointing*, 2011), and *Art Museums* (Blue Horse Press, 2014).

Michael N. Thompson likes bacon and fantasy football, but hates using ampersands. His poetry has appeared in numerous literary journals including *Word Riot, Toronto Quarterly* and *The Hobo Camp Review*. He is the author of four poetry collections, the most recent being *A Murder Of Crows* (University Of Hell Press, 2014). His next collection, *Days Of Swine and Roses,* will also be released through University Of Hell Press in 2017. His website is www.michaelnthompson.com

James Toupin, retired general counsel of the US Patent and Trademark Office, is a two-time Pushcart nominee, whose poems have appeared in numerous journals since he began publishing in 2008, most recently through *Virginia Quarterly Review* (online), *Beloit Poetry Journal, Beltway Poetry Quarterly*, Poecology and *First Class Literary Magazine.*

Travis Truax earned his bachelor's degree in English from Southeastern Oklahoma State University in 2010. His work has appeared in *Flyover Country, The Marathon Literary Review, The Flagler Review*, and *The Meadow.* After college he spent several years working in various national parks out west. He lives in Bozeman, Montana.

Gina Valdés work has been published in journals and anthologies in the U.S., Mexico, and Europe. She has recent or forthcoming work in *Huizache, Earth's Daughters*, and *Calyx.*

Milla van der Have (1975) wrote her first poem at 16, during a physics class. She has been writing ever since. In 2013 one of her short stories won a New Millennium Fiction Award. Publication credits include *Bare Hands Poetry, The Lindenwood Review, Off The Coast, Right Hand Pointing, Word Riot, Kentucky Review, The Meadow, Apeiron Review* and *Hermes Poetry Journal.* Milla lives and works in Utrecht, The Netherlands.

Loretta Diane Walker, a three time Pushcart nominee, has published three collections of poetry. Loretta was recently elected as Statesman in the Arts by Odessa's Heritage Council. Her manuscript *Word Ghetto* won the 2011 Bluelight Press Book Award. She teaches music in Odessa, Texas. Loretta received a BME from Texas Tech University and earned a MA from The University of Texas of the Permian Basin.

Allyson Whipple is a student in the online MFA program with the University of Texas at El Paso. She is the co-editor of the *Texas Poetry Calendar* and author of the chapbook *We're Smaller Than We Think We Are*. She teaches at Austin Community College.

Scott Wiggerman is the author of three books of poetry, *Leaf and Beak: Sonnets, Presence,* and *Vegetables and Other Relationships*; and the editor of several volumes, including *Wingbeats: Exercises & Practice in Poetry, Lifting the Sky: Southwestern Haiku & Haiga,* and *Wingbeats II.* Recent poems have appeared in *Naugatuck River Review, Red Earth Review, Pinyon Review, Borderlands: Texas Poetry Review,* and the anthologies *This Assignment Is So Gay, Forgetting Home: Poems about Alzheimer's,* and *The Great Gatsby Anthology.* He is an editor for Dos Gatos Press of Albuquerque, New Mexico.

Steve Wilson's work has appeared in journals and anthologies nationwide for the past thirty years. He is the author of three poetry collections – *Allegory Dance, The Singapore Express* and *The Lost Seventh* – and editor of *The Anatomy of Water: A Sampling of Contemporary American Prose Poetry.* He teaches in the creative writing program at Texas State University.

Clarence Wolfshohl lives with his writing, two dogs and one cat in a nine-acre woods outside of Fulton, Missouri. In late 2014, his chapbook *Equus Essence* was published online by Right Hand Pointing, and more recently his print chapbook *Chupacabra* by El Grito del Lobo Press (2015).

Christopher Woods is a writer, teacher and photographer who lives in Houston and Chappell Hill, Texas. He has published a novel, *The Dream Patch,* a prose collection, *Under a Riverbed Sky,* and a book of stage monologues for actors, *Heart Speak* His photographs can be seen in his gallery -http://christopherwoods.zenfolio.com/ He is currently compiling a book of photography prompts for writers, *From Vision to Text.*

Chila ("Sheila") **Woychik** is the owner and managing editor of Port Yonder Press. She loves nature and everything associated with it. She and her husband of a million years live on a small hobby farm in the Midwest. They have one grown son and a lovely daughter-in-law who live not so very far away. She's been published in print and online magazines many dozens of times and began writing in earnest in 1995. Her latest work appears in or is forthcoming in *Blueline, Silk Road, Emrys, Stoneboat, Pithead Chapel,* & others. Hobby-wise, she loves jeeping, hiking, animals, woods & stream, archery, boots, staying active, eating organic, and just ... well ... living. That may sound corny but she doesn't care. After a drunk driver hit her and her son head-on 10 years ago, each new day is so very special, and she's not afraid to say so.

Natalie Young is a founding editor for the poetry magazine *Sugar House Review.* By day, she works as an art director for a marketing firm based out of Salt Lake City. Previous publications include *Rattle, Tampa Review, Los Angeles Times, South Dakota Review, Green Mountains Review* and others. She is left-handed, half Puerto Rican and a fan of cottage cheese and The Muppets.

Paul Zarzyski is the recipient of the 2005 Governor's Arts Award for Literature. He received his MFA in creative writing from The University of Montana, where he studied with Richard Hugo. A bareback bronc rider, he's been a featured performer at the Elko Cowboy Poetry Gathering for the past 26 years, has toured Australia and England, and has recited at the National Book, Folk, and Storytelling Festivals, The ProRodeo Hall of Fame, The Library of Congress, The Kennedy Center Millennium Stage and with the Reno Philharmonic Orchestra. He was also featured in 1999 on Garrison Keillor's A Prairie Home Companion. His recent publications include *51: 30 Poems, 20 Lyrics, 1 Self Interview* (Bangtail Press, 2011). Born and raised in Hurley, Wisconsin, Paul has called Montana "home" since 1973.

As If Light Actually Matters

New and Selected Poems

Larry D. Thomas, 2008 Texas Poet Laureate

The present volume draws on nine book-length collections of Thomas's poetry, and includes a generous selection of new poems. Five of the collections are comprised of poems of geographic place, four of which are set primarily in Texas. His fifth "place" collection is set on the coast of Maine. The poems selected from his remaining collections range in subject matter from outlaw bikers to ekphrasis; from the avian world to an asylum for the criminally insane.

As If Light Actually Matters discloses a mind attuned to the flora and fauna of nature but also to the stark realities of the human condition. Thomas does not merely see what lies behind perception; he witnesses and transcribes that radiance, ensuring his abiding importance within American letters. As with contemporary poets such as Robert Morgan and the late James Wright, I consider Larry D. Thomas to be among the very best at his craft.

— William Wright, Senior Editor of *The Southern Poetry Anthology* Series; *Author of* Tree Heresies *and* Night Field Anecdote.

Texas Review Press. 978-1-68003-024-2 paper $12.95   978-1-68003-025-9 ebook 51/2x81/2. 200 pp.   Poetry.   April, 2015.

Woe to the Land Shadowing

Poems

Red Shuttleworth

Woe to the Land Shadowing
Poems
Red Shuttleworth

Red Shuttleworth's *Woe to the Land Shadowing* presents poems from the summer of 2015, from Washington State's worst fire season in history... new poems from the shrub steppe of the Columbia Basin north of Moses Lake.

Red Shuttleworth is a three-time recipient of the Spur Award (from Western Writers of America) for Poetry: *Johnny Ringo* (2013), *Roadside Attractions* (2011), and *Western Settings* (2001). Shuttleworth was named "Best Living Western Poet" in 2007 by *True West* magazine. His poetry and short plays have appeared in numerous journals, including *Alaska Quarterly Review, Concho River Review, Los Angeles Review, Ontario Review, Prairie Schooner, South Dakota Review,* and *Weber: The Contemporary West.* Shuttleworth's plays have been presented widely, including at The State University of New York at Fredonia, Sundance Playwrights Lab, The Sun Valley Festival of New Western Drama, and the Tony Award-winning Utah Shakespearean Festival.

A voice of the true West.
> *A true voice of the West.*
> — Adrian C. Louis, author of *Skins, Logorrhea,* and *Savage Sunsets*

Blue Horse Press. paper $12.00   978-0692560457 53 pp. Poetry. October, 2015.